# "Ambulance 464"
# Encore Des Blessés

THE AUTHOR WORKING ON HIS DIARY ON THE FRONT SEAT OF "464"

# "Ambulance 464"
# Encore Des Blessés
The experiences of an American Volunteer with the French Army during the First World War

Julien H. Bryan

*"Ambulance 464"*
*Encore Des Blessés*
*The experiences of an American Volunteer*
*with the French Army during the*
*First World War*
by Julien H. Bryan

First published under the title
*"Ambulance 464"*
*Encore Des Blessés*

Leonaur is an imprint
of Oakpast Ltd

Copyright in this form © 2010 Oakpast Ltd

ISBN: 978-0-85706-180-5 (hardcover)
ISBN: 978-0-85706-179-9 (softcover)

**http://www.leonaur.com**

Publisher's Notes

In the interests of authenticity, the spellings, grammar and place names used have been retained from the original editions.

The opinions of the authors represent a view of events in which he was a participant related from his own perspective, as such the text is relevant as an historical document.

The views expressed in this book are not necessarily those of the publisher.

# Contents

| | |
|---|---:|
| Preface | 9 |
| Introduction | 12 |
| Getting Ready | 15 |
| At Hill 304 and Mort Homme | 37 |
| In the Argonne Forest | 75 |
| "En Repos," and in Champagne | 94 |
| Coming Back | 118 |

To
My Mother and Father

# Preface

The American Ambulance Field Service was taken over by our army in France in October, 1917, and although many of its sections are still serving with the French forces it has lost its former identity. A few drivers remain, and several hundred have returned home; but the majority have joined some branch of the service with General Pershing's forces.

This book is an attempt to tell something of my own experiences as an ambulance driver with Section Twelve, and, at the same time, to give an idea of what the ambulance service is doing and will have to do probably for some time to come. It is my first book and has not been written without considerable effort, and I might even say sacrifice. Many a time last winter I scribbled in my diary until long after midnight, seated on a stretcher in my ambulance, with two kerosene lamps to give a little light and warmth.

I felt that I had a story to tell in my own way, and that, if necessary, I could revise it in a comparatively short time upon my return home. But the task has not been so easy as I imagined. I have spent many hours during the three months I have been at Princeton trying to put it into shape, and study and drill at the same time. I hope that I have succeeded. If I have, it is because I have tried to tell as simply as possible a few of the many things which happened in our section over there.

We of the American Ambulance Field Service have no desire to pose as heroes. I went over, as did so many of the others, with the object of seeing war at first hand and of getting some excitement, as well as being of some service. But we do not care to be talked of as young heroes trying to save France, because that was not our idea in going, at any rate not at first. But having arrived in France and learned of some of the terrible things which had been done by the enemy and what the French people had gone through, and having become imbued with some of the wonderful spirit of the French, our point of view was altered, and we were ashamed of our primary object in offering our services. Moreover, we realised on getting to the front that our own little section was but a single unit among the five million troops constituting the French army, and that individually we were very unimportant. Nevertheless, I hope we did our share in strengthening the morale of all those fine fellows with whom we came in contact. Seeing us Americans actually in the field with them doubtless inspired them with the hope that more would be coming over before long and they have not been disappointed.

I regret that I had to return before the war was over. I feel that I have gotten out of my work in France far more than I put into it. The experience and the life did me untold good and when my period of enlistment was up I would have stayed on and entered the Aviation Service had the decision been entirely my own. Family reasons necessitated my return home but I hope it will not be long before. I am again in the field of action.

In taking the photographs I used a postcard size camera, with a good anastigmatic lens, and I would advise anyone going over with the intention of taking pictures not to get a smaller camera, for although the larger size is occasionally troublesome, little pictures are always unsatisfactory. But this advice may be unnecessary, because our authorities, like the British, are very strict concerning the use of cameras within the war zone. Almost all our films were developed at the front, Gilmore and I using the loft of a barn for a laboratory, with buckets and basins for apparatus. Many were the negatives we spoiled when the weather was so cold that the developer would not act on the films. Sometimes we printed by sunlight and sometimes by means of the carbide headlights on one of the cars. I took about four hundred photographs altogether, and the best which survive are in this book.

I have also used a number of pictures taken by my friends, and wish to thank them for their kindness in giving me permission to do this. William Gilmore and Ray Williams, both of Section Twelve, supplied three and four, respectively, the latter number including the balloon pictures. Monsieur Bardellini took six of the pictures at Esnes and Colonel Thurneyssen the group of Boche prisoners. The Farnam, the bursting bomb, and Guynemer pictures I obtained from George Trowbridge.

I also have to thank Professor Harry Covington, of Princeton University, who very unselfishly devoted many hours of his valuable time in smoothing out rough places in the original manuscript. My sincere gratitude is likewise due to several friends who have very kindly helped me with suggestions, proof reading and numerous other details.

Julien H. Bryan.

February 14th, 1918.
65 Blair Hall,
Princeton, New Jersey.

# Introduction

When our President told us that the causes of the war were obscure and that the war did not concern us, he expressed the common feeling of the American people at the outbreak of the war. When in 1918 he told us that the object of the war was to make the world safe for democracy and only in the triumph of democracy could we expect peace, he expressed the common feeling of the American people at the present time. The difference between those two utterances indicates the distance which the American people had travelled during the three intervening years. The war has taught us something; it has taught us much. We now know as never before both the meaning and the value of democracy.

This volume affords a striking illustration of this change in the American point of view by portraying the change in a single mind and the causes which produced that change. Says the author in his preface:

> I went over, as did so many of the others, with the object of seeing war at first hand and of getting some excitement, as well as being of some service. But we do not care to be talked of as young heroes trying to save France, because that was not our idea in going, at any rate, not at first. But having arrived in France and learned of some of the terrible things which had been done by the enemy and what the French people had gone through, and having become imbued with some of the wonderful spirit of the French, we altered our point of view, and were almost ashamed of our primary object in offering our services. Moreover, we realized on getting to the front that our own little section was but a single unit among the five million troops constituting the French army, and that individually we were not very important.

The first of these lessons the American people have already learned; the second we are just beginning to learn.

Such a book as this has two distinct values.

It gives the reader at home a vivid picture of the scenes upon the field of battle. Such a book is all the better for not being literary. We get the first impressions of the actor not modified by the ambitions of a literary artist, and the effect of his artless narrative is all the greater because he has not in his mind the effect which he is trying to produce upon the reader. Simplicity, accuracy, and realism are his characteristics. He is so absolutely in the life that he has not in his mind the readers of the narrative.

And for this reason the book produces upon the reader an effect similar to that which the events produced on the writer. We also alter our point of view as he altered his. We wonder that we ever thought that this war did not concern us. We wonder that we ever thought of leaving our kin across the sea to fight for the world's freedom without our aid. The author tells us that by his experience he became imbued with some of the wonderful spirit of the French. In reading the story of his experiences we become imbued through him with some of the same wonderful spirit. The war is no longer three thousand miles away; it is at our doors. We also have passed through a kind of baptism of fire. And by our companionship with our fellow citizens on their field of battle we are inspired by their enthusiasm and nerved by their resolve to accept no peace which does not give us in the destruction of Prussian militarism a reasonable assurance that our sons will never have to take part in a like campaign.

Lyman Abbott.

Cornwall-on-Hudson, N.Y.

## ORIGINAL MEMBERS OF SECTION XII

| NAME | RESIDENCE IN AMERICA | COLLEGE |
|---|---|---|
| Allen, Wharton | Colorado Springs, Col. | Univ. of Penna |
| Benney, Philip* | Pittsburg | |
| Bryan, Julien H. | Titusville, Penna. | Princeton ('21) |
| Clark, Walter | Stockbridge, Mass. | |
| Cook, Robinson | Portland, Maine | Dartmouth |
| Craig, Harry W. | Cleveland, Ohio | Univ. of Wisconsin |
| Crowhurst, H. W., Jr. | Philadelphia | La Fayette |
| Dunham, Dowse | Irvington-on-the-Hudson | Harvard |
| Faith, Clarence | Nahant, Mass. | Tufts |
| Gillespie, James Park | East Orange | Yale |
| Gilmore, Wm. | Florence, Italy | "Boston Tech." |
| Haven, George | New York City | Yale |
| Houston, Henry H. | Philadelphia | Univ. of Penna. |
| Iselin, Harry | Normandy, France | |
| Kann, Norman | Pittsburg | "Carnegie Tech." |
| Keleher, Hugh | Cambridge, Mass. | Harvard |
| Lloyd, J. T. | Ithaca, N. Y. | Cornell |
| Lundquist, S. J. H. | San Francisco | |
| Orr, Thomas | Pittsburg | Hamilton |
| Powell, C. H. | Milwaukee | Univ. of Wisconsin |
| Walker, Croom | Chicago (and Alabama) | Univ. of Virginia |
| Williams, Ray Evan | Dodgeville, Wis. | Univ. of Wisconsin |

## MEN WHO JOINED THE SECTION AFTER WE LEFT PARIS

| NAME | JOINED IN | RESIDENCE IN AMERICA | COLLEGE |
|---|---|---|---|
| **Bradley, Lloyd P.** | Feb. | Berkeley, Cal. | Univ. of Cal. |
| Chauvenet, Louis | Feb. | St. Louis | Harvard |
| Coan, Raymond | March | N. Y. City (& Montclair) | Cornell |

*Benney entered Aviation in July and lost his life on January 25, 1918, while serving with the La Fayette Escadrille.

## MEN WHO JOINED THE SECTION AFTER WE LEFT PARIS
### Continued

| NAME | JOINED IN | RESIDENCE IN AMERICA | COLLEGE |
|---|---|---|---|
| Dixon, Philip | May | Milwaukee | Harvard |
| Harrison, W. Lyle | March | Lebanon, Ken. | Oberlin |
| Joyce, Thomas | May | Berkeley, Cal. | |
| Lloyd, J. T. | March | Ithaca, N. Y. | Cornell |
| O'Connor, Tom | May | Brookline, Mass. | |
| Sinclair, Gilbert | May | Minneapolis | Univ. Minnesota |
| Stanley, Everett | March | Milton, Mass. | Bowdoin |
| Tenney, Luman H. | March | Ada, Minnesota | Oberlin |

Ray Eaton }
Ellis Frazer } Three fictitious persons whom I have used here and there, when the mention of the real name has seemed unwise.
Mark Payne }

CHAPTER 1

# Getting Ready

*January 19th,* 1917.                    21 Rue Raynouard, Paris

Six weeks ago this morning, my alarm clock got me out of bed at five o'clock, in my little two by four room in the Erie Y. M. C. A. and off I rushed to my daily work, driving stakes and chaining track with the Engineering gang of the New York Central. It had all been very interesting for a few weeks after I left high-school last June. But after six long months it was becoming monotonous and I was aching to get away, to try my hand at something else. Since I was staying out of school for a whole year, waiting until I was eighteen before I entered college, it didn't take much to urge me on when I read a poster saying, "Volunteers Wanted for the American Ambulance Field Service in France." My father was enthusiastic about it. So immediately after the holidays, I left my home in Titusville, Pennsylvania, and sailed on the French liner *Espagne* on the eighth of January, along with twenty other fellows in the same service.

We had a wonderful trip, no submarines and very little unpleasant weather. Six of the men, including my cabin-mate, joined the Paris Service which works for the big American Ambulance Hospital in Neuilly. The rest of us went to the headquarters of the Field Service on Rue Raynouard, where we are now, waiting to be sent to the front. Soon several of the fellows will leave, to fill vacancies in one of the old sections. But there is a rumour going around that a new section, Number Twelve, is being organized and that our bunch is to be part of it. No wonder that we are all hoping that this is true, for it will be far better to go out with fellows whom we know than to break into the cliques of an old crowd.

We are living just across the river from the Eiffel Tower, in a won-

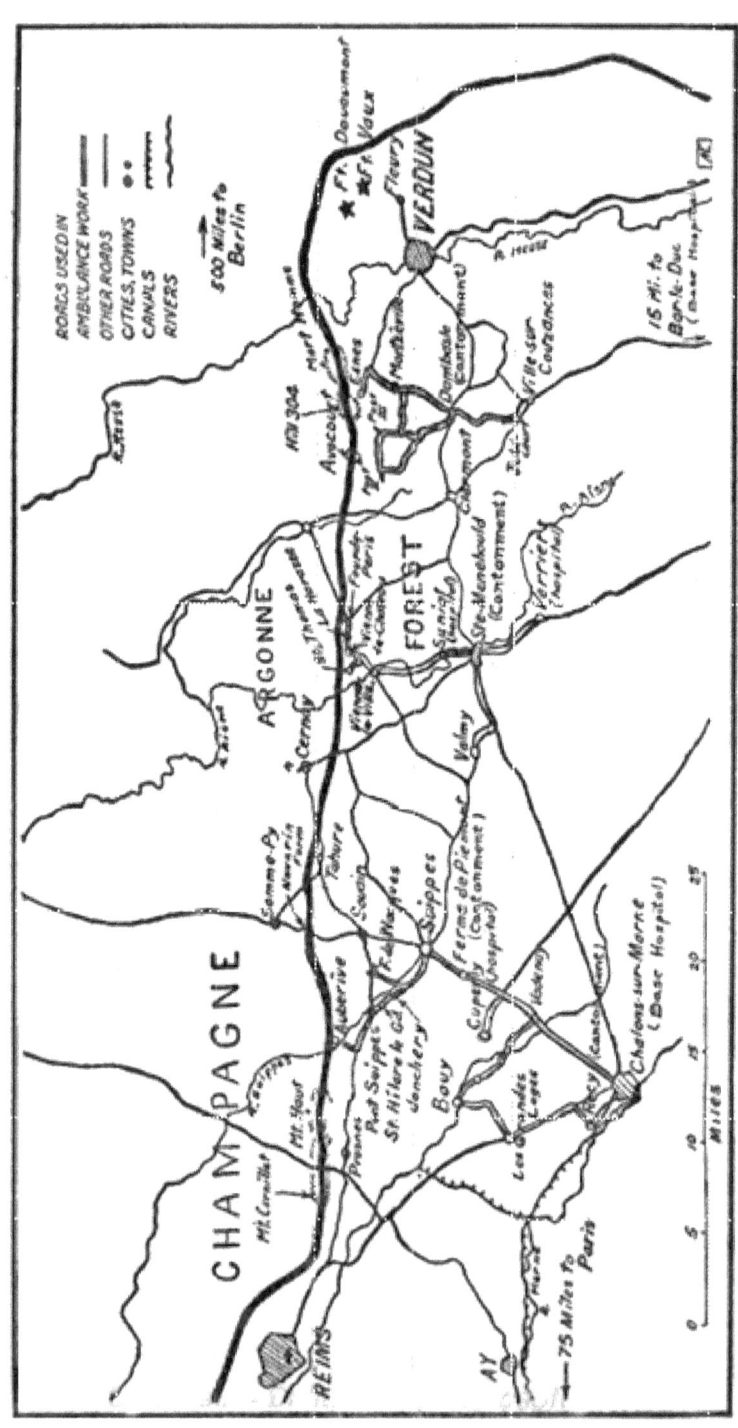

The Front from Reims to Verdun, where Section 12 worked

derful old house in Passy. Its grounds, which cover an entire block, have come down from the old Hottinguer and Bartholdi families. Ben Franklin, they tell us, used to stay here when he was in Paris and some of his first kite experiments were made in the park behind the house. All our quarters are downstairs and the upper part of the building has been turned into offices for the business end of the service. Dr. A. Piatt Andrew, Steven Galatti and Dr. Gros have separate offices here. Then there is the mailing department and Mr. Fisher's room, where we go to see about getting our necessary papers. The first thing we did on arriving yesterday was to report at the latter place to receive directions concerning the "*Permis de Sejour*" which we must get from the *Prefecture* of Police if we wish to remain in France.

Living in Paris just at present reminds one of the joys of an Arctic expedition. It's terribly cold, and raw and damp besides, and there is such a scarcity of coal that even after the government has carefully divided it among the inhabitants, there is just enough for a few hours' comfort and then a room at 45 or 50 degrees F. all the rest of the day. It is so bad in the quarters here that the ink has actually frozen in my suitcase. Every night there is a mad rush to undress as soon as we hit the bedroom and we make pretty good speed in dressing in the morning, too.

Whenever we feel we can't stand it any longer, we pay out fifteen *centimes*, about three cents in our money, for a ride in the subway which they call the *Metro*; they tell us it is the only warm place in Paris, in this, their coldest winter in twenty-seven years. The poor, of course, suffer the most. They can't afford to buy much coal when it sells for seventy dollars a ton. And so, daily, it is given out by a special card system at booths all over the city. Every morning crowds of poor women collect hours before the time of distribution, patiently wait their turn, and then go away one by one lugging a fifty-pound sack of the precious stuff.

*January 25th.* 21 Rue Raynouard, Paris.

Section Twelve is no longer a dream. All the necessary men are here and the twenty-two Fords have just had the last touches put on their ambulance bodies at Kellner's. We have no section leader or *chef*, as yet, nor have we been given our respective cars; but they tell us we will probably get our orders from the French Automobile Service to leave for the front next week. It won't be long before we get the cars.

From the stories of fellows who are in on permission from different parts of the front it appears that a Sanitary Section consists of twenty to twenty-five ambulances, each of which carries three stretcher or five sitting cases. There are also two big white trucks for supplies, extra parts, and the luggage of the eight Frenchmen who go along as mechanics, cooks and assistants in clerical work. Then they usually have two staff cars, one of which belongs to the *Chef Américain* and the other to the French lieutenant in charge of the Section. They live in a small town, often a destroyed one, between the front line trenches and the first hospitals in the rear; and for ordinary work they send about five men out each day for twenty-four hour duty at their different posts. These are little first aid stations, usually eight hundred or a thousand yards behind the first line trenches.

In hilly country, however, one can often go in a car to within four or five hundred yards of No Man's Land; but in level stretches like Champagne one seldom gets closer than two miles. The wounded are carried by stretcher bearers from wherever they have fallen to a tiny *Poste de Secours*, in the second or third line trenches. Here they are given quick treatment in the one-room underground hospital, and are rushed on afterwards through the communication trenches to one of our posts. These are underground, too, and are little better than the posts in the trenches. But they can handle more men here and do emergency work, like amputating, if necessary. Besides, when a big attack is on, *blessés* are brought in much faster than we can remove them and they take care of them here for a few hours, and sometimes for days if necessary.

Our work is to load up the ambulances with the assistance of the *brancardiers* (stretcher-bearers) and carry them back to an evacuation hospital ten or twelve miles behind the lines. These are rather crude affairs and seldom employ any women nurses. When they become crowded or get cases too difficult to handle, they send the wounded to bigger hospitals further back, usually in a nearby city. Such places are twenty-five or thirty miles behind the front and are very similar to our base hospitals. From here patients are sent by train into Paris for major operations or to the south of France to recuperate.

Mr. Fisher took five of us out in the Ford truck Tuesday morning and gave us a short driving-lesson in anticipation of the final test for the French driver's license which we must have before we go to the front. It was comparatively simple for most of us; but some real excitement started when Payne, one of the Espagne men, started driving. He is sort of a queer duck, anyway. The first night he was in Paris he crawled over the picket fence around the Eiffel Tower and was almost shot by a sentry.

He did nobly on Tuesday, however. He had barely taken the wheel before we saw that he had never driven much before. He jammed on the accelerator just as we were rounding a corner, headed for a tree, and unfortunately missed it by a few inches, or we would have stopped here. Then he speeded up considerably, and skidded for thirty feet along a trolley-track embankment, scraped the side of an old dray horse and then ducked under its nose just for spite. We finally ended up two miles further on, with Mr. Fisher hanging firmly to the wheel and doing his best to get Payne's feet off the pedals so that he could use his own and stop the machine. . . . Payne now thinks he ought to have another practice lesson before he goes to the front. We agree with him.

We were given the second dose of typhoid and para-typhoid bugs today. Dr. Gros stuck something like a billion and a half in each fellow's arm and we certainly knew afterwards that they were having a grand time all by themselves in there. Everybody feels rotten and some of the men have gone to bed already, although it is only seven thirty. It is *para*-T, not typhoid itself which makes one's arm so sore a few hours after the injection.

When we first got here, we could do pretty much as we pleased, as long as we saw about our papers and had our uniforms made. But now that the Section is going to leave soon, and since they are shorthanded at Kellner's anyway, the whole bunch goes out there every afternoon and unpacks and mounts Ford chassis. Women and children flock around in swarms whenever we are working on the crates. They watch us like hawks, eager to seize the tiniest splinter which may fall from a broken board. They figure that one good-sized basket of chips will cook a supper which otherwise they would have had to eat cold. We used to sightsee a little mornings: but every big thing like the Louvre and the Eiffel Tower is closed for the duration of the war and it isn't very interesting wandering around the outside of buildings. Entertainment in the evening is not difficult, for many of the big theatres and both the Opera and Opera Comique are still running.

Anderson, my roommate on the Espagne, who is now at Neuilly, and I have gone three times already to the Opera, where we saw *Manon* and *L'Etranger*. The music was wonderful but I think we enjoyed the comfortable warmth of the building almost as much. Everyone goes, from the poor *poilu*, in on a few days' furlough, who listens enraptured from his two-*franc* seat in the fourth balcony, to the bemedalled Russian and Italian officers, who, as guests of the French Republic, occupy the seats in the orchestra circle far below. There are usually many women in the audience, but most of them are widows: at least you seldom see one who isn't in mourning for a brother, a son or a husband. . . . Broadway is still lit up after the theatres are out, but here everything is dark. It is against the law to use electricity for illuminating signs or store-windows. I have noticed that some of the fashionable shops are using long tapering candles which probably burn out by themselves in the early hours of the morning.

*January 31st.*

Today we started all the new ambulances and drove them down into the park below the house. Here they were carefully lined up and examined to see that no part of the equipment was missing. Then after dinner Mr. Fisher assigned each one of us to a car and gave us its number. Mine turned out to be four hundred and sixty-four, and the name plate on its side read "Schenectady Ambulance." It was very kind of the people in Schenectady to donate the machine, but it is certainly a terrible pet name for an automobile to have. There are a lot of Americans who don't know how to pronounce the word Schenectady, to say nothing of the queer noises the Frenchmen make trying to say it. Already it has been called everything from Shenickadaydy to Skinneckodidy.

The motor seems to be ok. I took it around the block for a trial run after dinner and had no trouble with the engine. A taxi collided with me up on Rue Raynouard, however, when I was completing the test, and smashed in my side-box pretty badly. The big machine turned from a narrow alley into the main street without sounding its horn and I couldn't stop in time after I saw it. The damage done was very slight, and it will only need a new box which can be easily replaced.

I wore my uniform for the first time this morning. It gives you the most wonderful feeling to be able to ride in the Metro and walk around down town without having every soul in Paris stare at you as if you were some terrible slacker.

*February 5th,* 1917.                              Still at 21 Rue Raynouard.

They gave us our chef the day before yesterday. He is Harry Iselin of Section Two; and tonight, they had the farewell banquet in honour of Section XII. Dr. Gros and Dr. Andrew both made interesting speeches afterwards. Mr. Simonds, War Correspondent of the New

1. THE REMAINS OF TWO AMBULANCES, DESTROYED BY GERMAN SHELL-FIRE. *THEY WERE BROUGHT INTO PARIS TO ENCOURAGE THE NEW ARRIVALS.*
2. THE TWENTY-ONE AMBULANCES OF SECTION 12, ASSEMBLED IN THE YARD AT 21 RUE RAYNOUARD
3. ONE OF THE MANY TOWNS WHICH THE BOCHES LEVELLED TO THE GROUND IN 1914.

1. Winter sport washing our cars in the River Couzances at Jubécourt.
2. Three little residents of "Rat-hunt" alley, in Jubécourt. All have hobnails in their shoes.
3. Ten miles behind the lines, in our dining room, the cowstable in Jubécourt. Every evening a few *poilus* dropped to sing and tell stories with us.

York *Tribune*, spoke for a few minutes, and after him came the finest talk of the evening, perhaps the most touching words I have ever heard. It was given by Monsieur Hughes Le Roux, a famous French journalist and adventurer. He told us in almost perfect English how he had lost both of his sons early in the war and he bravely described how one had died and how he had barely managed to get to his bedside and hear the story from his own lips before he passed away. He showed us why the work of the American Ambulance meant so much to him and he made every man who had come from a mere desire for adventure, feel that it was really his duty to help France. A few toasts to the two nations followed this, and with them came the end of a pleasant evening.

Every time I start a letter home something unexpected happens and I put it off another day. Yesterday when I was reading the Paris Edition of the New York *Herald*, I got so interested in the account of our probable break with Germany that I bought a *Daily Mail* and a *Matin* besides, and spent all the time when I should have been writing, bickering with the fellows over the news. Then on Friday the new men from the liner *Chicago* arrived and when I was introduced to one of my cousins from Pittsburg whom I hadn't known was coming over, I didn't bother with letter-writing any more that day. Unfortunately he was seized with pneumonia yesterday on his way back from Bordeaux in a convoy of Fords. He is now in a serious condition at the American Hospital in Neuilly. His chances are said to be about even. Bliss, another ambulance man, died last week from the same disease.

The "*Ordre de Mouvement*" for the Section has just come. Unless the Eiffel Tower falls on our cars during the night, we shall leave here at noon tomorrow.

*Thursday, Feb. 8th*, 1917.                                         Montmirail

Section 12 left its comfortable (?) quarters in Rue Raynouard today, after a grand review and military send off by Capitaine Aujay, the Frenchman who directs all the automobile work in Paris. He delivered a thrilling speech in French which none of us understood until it was carefully interpreted afterwards.

It took us several hours to get out of Paris, for we had to go eastward across the whole city. Several of the cars had engine trouble and one received a bad bump from a street car. Otherwise nothing unusual happened. By the time we came to Champigny, a little village twenty kilometres from the city, it was noon, and we stopped there for lunch.

It was a funny meal, served in a queer little café. First a loaf or so of stale bread and some wine appeared and after a long wait some prime ribs of horse. This appeared to be the last course, but as we were about to leave, in came a plate of rice and a minute later some cheese and jam.

In the afternoon we started up at a faster pace than before, with orders to keep the cars about fifty yards apart. It was extremely cold, and the bitter wind, which was blowing directly against us, seemed to go right through our heavy mackinaws. Now and then someone would stop, to change a spark plug or a tire, or perhaps to put in a little oil. Often, when he tried to pass another machine in order to get back to his old position in the convoy, a heated scrap would arise. Sometimes they raced for two or three miles, trying to push each other off the road. And before the afternoon was over, the cars were strung out in a line four miles long, with each driver jealously guarding his position while he kept it, and madly attempting to get it back again if it were taken away.

It was quite dark when we entered Montmirail, but we could not help seeing the ghastly ruins of the place, which the Germans had levelled in their advance before the Battle of the Marne. The staff car, which had gone on ahead, found an old dance hall where we could spend the night, and a place nearby in which to park our cars. We drained our radiators hurriedly, and had supper at a little cafe. Then as soon as we got back to quarters most of us took our blankets from our cars, and turned in without undressing.

*Saturday, Feb. 10th.*                                               Longeville.
I learned a hard lesson last night about sleeping. Never make your bed on a slope. I had fixed mine on the straw, with one end considerably lower than the other, and when I awoke this morning I was actually five feet lower down the hill than when I went to sleep. I had, moreover, slipped out into the cold air half a dozen times during the night.

It was mighty hard work starting the cars this morning, on account of the stiffness of the motors and the extreme cold. There were a number which we could not start at all by cranking, and we were obliged to tow them up and down the road in high speed, until they were warmed up. This took some time and it was almost eleven o'clock before we left the village.

Late in the afternoon we stopped outside of Bar-le-Duc and were delayed there thirty minutes because of a long convoy of supply wagons which had just entered the city. We thought we heard some big guns in the distance while we waited and a number of aeroplanes flew overhead. Two or three were low enough to enable us to see the red, white and blue targets on each wing. All of the Allied planes use this as an identification mark. Now we entered the town, and everyone, feeling tired and hungry, thought that our drive was over. There was no room for us in Bar-le-Duc, however, and we had to push on to a little place called Longeville: and although it was only five kilometres off, it was as tiresome a ride as I have ever taken.

We left the machines at length in a muddy side-street for the night, and then wandered off to get our supper and straw for bedding.

*Monday, Feb. 14th.*                                               Longeville.

We slept in an old barn to which we had been detailed the first two nights, but the close atmosphere drove us to our cars. I have made a regular little cabin out of mine. A good-sized bundle of straw, spread over the floor of the car, makes a fine mattress and for my heating and lighting system I have two kerosene lanterns. I am writing now sitting up in bed, and with my mackinaw on, since the heaters are not always too efficient. Pretty soon it will become stuffy and then I will throw back the canvas flap and the side windows and go to sleep.

On Monday we shifted all the cars to a new parking place behind the village church. Iselin had us move them here so that we might have a better location in case we were not ordered to move immediately.

Yesterday I saw a wedding in this church. It was a sad affair. The bride was a great, strong peasant woman and the groom a sickly, little chap who could not get into the army. The whole bridal party, father, mother and all the relatives were dressed in deep mourning and the only happy persons in the entire church were the altar boys who played tug of war with the priest's robe and fought over the stick in the incense pot.

The food is much better now. We have taken possession of the *café* near the canal and have rigged up a temporary kitchen in the woodshed. Harry ran across the Quaker Oats box recently and every morning we have oatmeal which is a lot better than prune jam on stale army bread. This bread is certainly remarkable stuff. It comes in freight cars from the interior and is usually two weeks old before we get it. It is often brittle, like a piece of wood, and is about as palatable as soft pine. However, it is supposed to be nourishing and I think that it is really more wholesome than our own American white bread.

*Tuesday, Feb. 20th.*                    Longeville, awaiting orders.

We have been attached to a division, the 132nd, so the lieutenant told us tonight. It is only a few miles away, near Brillon, and tomorrow or the next day a few cars will be called out to do evacuation work. I presume it will be to carry a few sick or accident cases and perhaps to get acquainted with the different regiments of the division. Everyone is working hard on his car so that it may be in tiptop shape if he is detailed to go. It will be a great relief to have something to do. So far we have just hung around the café, waiting for the next meal to come. We play poker, read, or practice French on the cook; and once or twice a day the mandolin and the guitar get going and we have some singing. And if you grow tired of sitting indoors all day, you can take long walks among the hills overlooking Bar-le-Duc and the Ornain. But even this has become tiresome and we joyfully welcome the idea of getting to work.

I was very dirty when I finished going over my car and since I had not washed for five or six days, I filled my basin full of nice hot radiator water and took an outdoor bath. The weather was quite chilly and before I had finished a group of wondering children had gathered around. They were amazed that anyone should wash in the open or even bother with keeping clean at all in such weather. I shall never forget how they looked in their black aprons with their clumsy school packs hanging over their shoulders, as they stood beside my car. I pestered them with simple little questions, just to help my French; and oh, how they laughed when they found I didn't know an easy word like "cat" or "barn."

Almost every day now we hear the big guns along the Saint Mihiel sector; and tonight some very heavy shelling is going on. The nearest guns are about twenty miles away.

I tried developing a few films last evening in the loft in the barn. It was certainly working under difficulties. The temperature of the room was a couple of degrees below freezing and although I had some lukewarm water when I started, it went down to forty five degrees while the films were developing. Of course, I spoiled a number of mighty good pictures which I had taken on the ride out from Paris. I managed to save just two or three mediocre negatives out of the whole lot.

We got our gas masks and helmets today. I came a little late and had to be content with a big affair which comes way down over my ears.

*February 26th,* 1917. Within 464, Longeville.

"Ott" Kann and Gilmore have just left the car. We have been enjoying a delightful afternoon tea together, consisting of sardines, *petit beurre* and Radiator Water Cocoa. The latter we made by running the motor fast for a few minutes until the water began to boil and then pouring it into a cup of prepared powdered chocolate. Aside from the mineral water flavour, it was very good.

On Thursday we had our first evacuation work. I rode along with Cook to learn the roads to the different villages in which the division is stationed. We drove to Brillon which is about eight kilos from Bar-le-Duc and finding no cases there we went on to Haironville where we picked up two *assis* (sitting cases) and a *couché* (a stretcher case). The latter was in bad shape and we had to drive back very carefully. We dropped all three cases at the big hospital in Bar, and then speeded home by the canal road.

I drove Number 148, the supply car, today to get the section *ravitaillement* from the military storehouse near the Railroad station. We were obliged to wait an hour and a half to get our rations of bread, *pinard*, cheese and meat and a small box of coal for the kitchen. The engine got cold in the meanwhile and I had quite a time starting it. The old bus is in bad shape anyway, for the brake band is about worn off and I can't go into reverse at all. After dinner I wrote a long letter home. Phillipe, the French sergeant saw it and made me mail it in two separate envelopes. There is some military rule that no letter shall weigh over twenty grams, the equivalent of about four average sheets.

*Tuesday, Feb. 27th.* The Same.

My first real trip alone was successful. I took the flivver to Bar this afternoon and from there over the hills to Lisle-en-Rigault. They wanted me to take seven *assis* here and though five is usually our limit, I crowded six inside and had one sit up in front with me. Counting myself, this made eight people which is a pretty heavy load for any Ford, especially for one of our ambulances with its long overhanging body. However, it pulled very well over the bumpy little road leading to the main, Bar-le-Duc to St. Dizier, highway. As usual, since they were all *malade* cases, I left them at the H. O. E. in Bar. Then I had to return to Lisle and go on from there to Saudrupt where there was an officer with a severe case of mumps. While he was getting ready to

1. Section 12 making a short halt, while in convoy from Dombasle to Waly.
2. The old church at Dombasle. The images escaped unharmed in the bombardment.
3. Our quarters or cantonment in Dombasle. We have the best house in the village.

1. Road repairers at work, cleaning up the ruins of Dombasle. They tear down the walls and use the debris to fill up the ruts.
2. Ray Williams of Wisconsin, next to a "Put out your lights" sign, about eight miles from the front lines.
3. Camouflage on the Esnes road, screening us from Mort Homme.

leave, I got into conversation with some *poilus* standing near. Several of them had studied English in school and most of them knew a little German.

We got along remarkably well and I was greatly surprised to learn that they did not object to speaking *allemand*, as they call German. One young chap became quite interested when he learned that I was an American (everyone around here believes that we are English, on account of our uniforms) and after giving me his name and address, made me promise to write to him. Tony Cucuron was his name. He was rather surprised when I told him that we were volunteers; but when I said that we not only received no pay except the *poilus'* five cents a day, but had paid our own passage over and had bought all our equipment ourselves, he wouldn't believe me. He could not understand why we should leave our pleasant homes in America to come into a war like this, even though it were to help France.

Crowhurst, the mechanic, ground down 148's valves today and also scraped out the carbon. Afterwards he did the same thing to Powell's car. Most of the others, however, he won't have to touch for some time yet.

This afternoon Williams and I walked into town. We wandered around for some time, until a *patisserie* with some pretty cream tarts in the window, caught our eye. We spent all we could afford here. Just after we left we ran across a couple of Section 4 men. They are having some heavy work up in the Argonne, about fifty kilometres north of here and not far from Clermont.

Iselin was not feeling well when he went the rounds with the *mèdecin chef* today and when he came in tonight they found he had scarlet fever. Benney took him into the hospital in Bar where he will be well taken care of. Everyone is quite worried about it, however, for not only may the stuff spread through the section, but we will be without a chef for five or six weeks; and this is rather a serious loss, because we are very likely to move up to the front in a few days and one of us will have to take charge.

*February 28th.* Hotel "Barn" at Vadélaincourt.
Farewells were said to Longeville and the old *café* this morning. We headed directly north on the Verdun Road and pretty soon we began to see things we had read about at home. Here were the remains of a village, shot to pieces in 1914. The streets were quiet. Not a soul was left in the place. Again we would pass a group of young German pris-

oners with P. G. (*prisonnier de guerre*) written in huge letters on their backs; or perhaps some imported "Indo-China" labourers at work repairing the road. Once in a while a big gun would boom northeast of us. Now and then we would see a group of aeroplane hangars with their audiphones and anti-aircraft "seventy-fives."

But the most interesting thing of all was when we stopped at a cross-road to watch one of our regiments go by. They were marching slowly when they drew near, for their packs were heavy and they had been walking steadily since sunrise. But the fine young manhood which fills the ranks of our own army was no longer there. Here was a lad of seventeen, barely able to walk twenty miles a day, let alone to carry his sixty pounds of equipment that distance; and beside him strode a tall gaunt man of forty whom the long march had fatigued even more than it had the youth. As they passed us, their band broke out with a lively air and every soldier there straightened up immediately, and unconsciously quickened his step. And I shall never forget how they cheered and sang when the band played the "*Marseillaise*." Company after company took up the strain, and before long it had spread far down the valley, to the other end of the regiment.

We entered Vadélaincourt about noon and parked our cars at the entrance of the big aviation field there. Two minutes after we arrived every fellow in the section was out exploring the grounds. There were no officers around and since the workmen seemed to have no objections to our examining the machines, we went into every hangar and looked them all over. There were only three types here, the Farnam observation plane, and two fast little machines, the Spad and Nieuport. All of these were biplanes but some distance down the hill were six or seven monoplane tents. Lundquist and Gilmore got a couple of empty bombs as souvenirs. They are a yard long, look like great steel cigars, and are rather awkward to carry around.

The guns sound extremely clear now. We are about fifteen kilometres from Verdun and ten from at all the little earthquake which shook all their belongings down from the rack on top of them. Ten minutes later when the *pajama* clad athlete emerged from his cabin again and tried his dash over the roofs of the cars for the second time, his former victims were ready for him and he was obliged to make a hasty retreat through a "*tir de barrage*" of soft mud and snow.

Although we can't sleep in the old stable we have fixed up a dining-room and kitchen there. In the former we have two stoves and some tables and benches which we made from the planking of the second floor. And since there are really no more *malades* to carry here than before, we spend most of our time in this room.

Two German planes crossed the lines today in the direction of Bar. But they soon changed their direction when the French anti-aircraft guns began to pepper them. They were up almost twelve thousand feet, slightly out of range, I think. It was most interesting to watch the shrapnel break into great puffs of white smoke, sometimes rather near them but more often a long way off. I guess the guns do little more than keep them high up: and one of the Frenchmen said that the seventy-five nearest us had brought down only one German machine during the whole war.

Besides our dining room tables we have put up two stoves in the centre of the room. The larger of these makes ideal toast out of army bread which we find loses much of its oak-like firmness and becomes fairly palatable when cooked this way. But, as so frequently happens in America, a company has been formed which has a complete monopoly on the toast producing parts of the stove. The Jubécourt "Toast Trust" as the organization is called, is composed of six members. Every day before each meal one of them saunters in and takes possession of the army bread refinery. He starts work immediately and makes about twice as much toast as they need. It is rather slow work and the independent companies seldom get a show before the meal is half done. Occasionally when a director of the trust gets careless and leaves a vacant place, one of the outsiders sneaks on a fresh piece of bread. Then when he goes away, he takes two or three pieces and the trust wants to sue him for trespassing and burglary.

"I'll have to stop writing now. My lamp has been flickering for some time, and now it has gone out entirely.

*March 8th,* 1917.                                  Still in Jubécourt.

To the tune of a mouth organ attempting everything from "Melody in F" to "*O, du lieber Augustine*," and the noise issuing from a stud poker game going on at the other end of the room, I sat down to write this evening. It is pretty bad here, but worse in my own car. Five new men came yesterday to take the places of some of our fellows who are sick. Powell and Haven have pneumonia and Harry Iselin is still ill with scarlet fever. And since there are always a couple of chaps laid up with *grippe* or tonsilitis, we can make good use of them.

Today we had for breakfast what André, the cook, calls "Quawcour Ats"—(oatmeal). This was followed by the usual stale bread and jam.

About once a week we get a little butter, and last Sunday morning we were given one fried egg apiece upon a square inch of ham. I believe I enjoyed it more than any meal I have ever eaten. For dinner we had some rather tough Irish stew, which André says he used to make for Baron Rothschild, with *pinard* and cheese for dessert. Supper was a three course meal with army bread soup, boiled lentils (a concoction which tastes likes oats), and chocolate mush as the big items.

I have just returned from the regular nightly rat hunt. It is a pastime not very well known in America but very popular here at the front. Every evening we collect our clubs and flashlights and raid an old barn near the river. Two or three of us usually rush in together, flash our lights about until we spot a rat and then fall upon it with our sticks. It takes a good clean shot to kill one and we consider ourselves lucky if we get two or three in an evening.

*March 11.*                      Inside "Shenickadaydy" Jubécourt.

You can talk all you want about the good old spreads at boarding school and college, but when you put five husky young fellows, two gasoline blowtorches, three bottles of champagne and every edible from canned chicken to welsh rarebit into one little Ford ambulance you come pretty close to approaching the infinity of fun. This was the kind of celebration we had tonight in Gilmore's car; and it lasted until the early hours of the morning. There were Lundquist and Dunham, Chauvenet and Gilmore, and I, packed into the rear end of 443. It was the queerest party I have ever attended. In the first place our legs were all tied together in a knot in the centre. Gilmore himself, owner of the banquet hall and master of ceremonies sat at one end and made army bread toast for the Welsh rarebit. He cooked it on a piece of brass shell casing, hammered out flat, with the blowtorch underneath it to supply the heat. Lundquist mixed the egg sauce for the lobster salad, while Dunham opened the cans of sardines, peas, and chicken.

Chauvenet had to test the champagne after he had uncorked one bottle and my job was to butter the hardtack which we had stolen from the kitchen, and also to see that the smaller torch which was boiling the water for the chocolate didn't tip over into Lundquist's lap. We ate course after course of stuff which Gil had gotten at some time or other from the *epicerie*. But cocoa, lobster, champagne, welsh rarebit, peas and hardtack don't work too well together, the bunch became more and more uproarious, and the party almost ended in a rough and tumble contest with the lighted lamps as weapons.

1. Morning exercise in front of the "Poste de Secours" in Montzèville. The dugout is on the right.
2. Four Boche "iso's" (6 in. shells) exploding behind some carefully concealed batteries near Montzèville, after passing directly over our heads.
3. Afternoon tea at Post Two in the Bois (forest) d'Avocourt. We sleep in the shelter behind the four poilus. My car is in the background.

1. The *Château* at Esnes. Behind it lies Hill 304. Our post was in the wine-cellars underneath. In the foreground are six wooden crosses.
2. A caisson for "75" shells, which a Boche shell finished near the church.
3. The ruins of the church in Esnes.
4. The road through the village. The water is a foot deep in places here and conceals all the fresh shell holes.

General N——, the commander of our division, passed through the village this afternoon and reviewed the section. Our orders were to stand motionless beside our cars and to look straight ahead. But the general was a good natured old fellow and spoke to several of the men as he passed, instead of marching formally by, funeral fashion. If they do any attacking, he will lead the 132nd when they go up to the front.

CHAPTER 2

# At Hill 304 and Mort Homme

*March 14th*, 1917.               Our last day at Jubécourt.
At last the good news has come. Tomorrow morning we are to end this lazy existence and take Section One's place at Dombasle. This afternoon, the *Mèdecin Chef* piled ten of us into two ambulances and took us over some roads north of Dombasle which we will use in our work there. A few miles from Jubécourt we found ourselves in a thick wood which my map called "Bois d'Avocourt." Soon we veered off sharply to the left, onto a bumpy road where there was barely room for two cars to pass. All the *camions* and munition wagons are forced to use it because the Boches have the exact range of the main route and pepper it continually. Suddenly, as we were passing a couple of bomb-proofs or *abris*, a terrific explosion sounded behind us and for a minute we thought it was a Boche shell arriving; but three more bangs followed shortly and we soon learned that it was a battery of 155's at work. Here we were, literally on top of a battery of 6 inch guns which the Germans battered daily, as we could tell by the splintered trees and numerous shell holes.

Yet they were so cleverly concealed that even when they were fired, all that we could see was the flame from the mouth of the gun. We went on to three or four "*Postes de Secours*" to which we will come soon for twenty-four hour stretches, waiting for wounded and carrying them when they arrive to some hospital ten or twelve miles in the rear. At one place about a mile from the front line trenches, where we stopped for a few minutes, Crowhurst and Faith stumbled into a pile of heavy iron balls with queer caps attached. They carried three or four along for several miles, only to learn later from one of the Frenchmen that they were hand grenades, and would explode in eight seconds after the cap was touched. Here and there we encountered a fresh shell hole in the road and even oftener the traces of an old one which had been filled with crushed stone. Luckily no shells fell near us today but the fellows in another car who took a different road said they had some narrow escapes. I found out later that they always tell you this.

We held an informal reception in the barn tonight after the rat hunt. Some of the Frenchmen in the village dropped in and told several mighty interesting stories about their experiences in the war. I couldn't understand a great deal but I remember they talked a lot about the inside story of the second Battle of Verdun, and the sacrifices the French made to keep Douaumont and Vaux. Then they switched to the very beginning of the war, when the Germans first violated the Red Cross laws by concealing machine guns in their ambulances and driving them up to No Man's Land, seemingly to collect wounded after an attack. After this ambulances were not allowed to go up to the first lines. I only wish that I knew more French for there were lots of interesting points that I missed entirely.

When the party finally broke up, Benney and I went outside to watch the star shells bursting nine miles away, around Avocourt and Hill 304. It is quite a sight to watch them shoot up into the heavens, break forth in a brilliant magnesium light and then slowly descend in a parachute until the flame dies down. I don't suppose we will be so fond of them though, when we get in among them.

Some Titusville *Heralds* came today and I enjoyed the rural news especially. If I recall correctly, Samantha Babbs of Porkey had an earache and the Royal Order of Oil Creek Township Owls had their annual meeting. Wiener sandwiches and *sauerkraut* were served by the young ladies of the Female Department.

*St. Patrick's Day.*                          Donbasle-en-Argonne

I am sitting before a fire in our quarters. It is quite a hot one for I have just put on the legs of an old oak bedstead and the polished top of a wrecked mahogany writing-desk. They burn well and make it much pleasanter here than it was at Jubécourt. Besides, ours is the best house remaining in the village. Practically all of the others fell in ruins during a heavy bombardment last fall. With the exception of a few road-menders we are the sole occupants of the place. The peasants were all forced to flee after the shelling. I understand that the Germans still punish it quite regularly. Naturally our life here ought to be interesting.

When we arrived last Thursday, all of Section One's cars were lined up in the road opposite the cantonment and we had barely time to say "Hello" before they were speeding down the road towards Vadélaincourt. They will be *en repos* there for a couple of weeks. Then came a general scramble for rooms. Bradley and I stuck together and found a wonderful little shack behind the main building. We didn't have possession long, however, for our French Lieutenant had previously chosen it and we were forced to give it up to him. We tried the parlour of the big house after this. It was pretty good except that the ceiling had recently fallen and left several inches of debris on the floor. But this was fine compared to the rooms some of the other fellows had. We went vigorously to work and in two hours had a fairly respectable place for our stretchers. Just after we had finished, two slackers joined us and we ended with a merry party of six in our parlour.

Yesterday morning Ott Kann was on duty at Montzèville and I went out with him to learn the road. It is sort of a relay or half way post between Dombasle and Esnes; and although Esnes is a mile and a half closer to the trenches, still Montzèville gets a good many *blessés* from the batteries and engineer's posts nearby. The town is in a much worse condition than Dombasle. Hardly a wall remains and the few soldiers who stay in the place, live deep underground in *abris*. We left Ott's blanket roll in the "*Poste de Secours*" and then climbed out into the open again to look around a little. We had just emerged when a terrific screech like the tearing of an enormous piece of cloth, sounded above us, a violent explosion occurred in the road in front of us and little stones and *éclat* came pattering down all around, but not before we had tumbled headlong down the *abri* entrance and were safe underground once more.

Three more shells fell outside and then, when nothing else happened for some time, we got our nerve back again and crawled slowly out. We poked around the ruins for a while until we got some distance from the post. Here on top of a pile of stones, once the walls of a little cottage, we gazed at the distant summit of a hill where French shells were breaking instead of German. For the enemy held the crest. This was the famous *Mort Homme*. Craig stopped by soon after this on his way to Esnes, and since Ott was on twenty-four hour duty here and there was no point in my staying with him, I went on with Craig, to learn the road.

It was late in the afternoon when we got started. Immediately upon leaving the village we came into plain sight of the trenches. However, it happened that we were seen far more clearly by the enemy than we could possibly see him. We had to drive over an exposed road along the brow of a hill with the fields on either side of us speckled with shell-holes. Opposite us were the Boche trenches showing up in thin, white lines, which were occasionally marked by a puff of smoke from an exploding seventy-five. I experienced the same, shivery feeling here which one often has at home, before getting up to make a speech in school. You try to tell yourself everything is all right, but still you seem to quiver all over. However, from the glances I stole at Craig now and then, I knew that he was just as worked up as I was. This idea seemed to cheer me immensely and I felt much more at ease afterwards.

We drove into Esnes, the little town where we have our "*Poste de Secours*," just after sunset, and what had once been peaceful homes rose before us in shattered walls and ugly piles of stones. In the whole place there was no building with its sides still intact, and very few which had any walls at all. It can never hope to be rebuilt. We were forced to drive slowly through the town, for barbed wire, waiting to be hauled to the trenches, lay about in huge piles, sometimes projecting out into the street; and big logs, to be used for dugout supports, were scattered about. Half a dozen fresh shell holes and an occasional arrive a hundred yards or so away added to the pleasure of the trip.

We finally got to the old *château* where the post is located and had barely climbed out of the car when one of the stretcher-bearers met us, and said two *couchés* were waiting. We carefully put them in, the *brancardiers* helping, and then in the dusk drove back with them to the hospital at Ville. Craig went pretty slowly, in fact, the whole distance in low speed, but the poor chaps moaned all the way.

Clark certainly has hard luck. Last night he was driving along the Post Two road in the Bois d'Avocourt when he got stuck in a bad mud hole and had to wait there three hours before any help came. Just as he started on his way again a "210" exploded in the road, forty feet in front of him, splashed mud all over him and shook the whole car. He stopped and sat there shaking, he said, for five or ten minutes. Finally he got his nerve back and went on to Ville sur Couzances, to the H. O. E. And after all this, when he was sitting before the fire in his quarters tonight, his roommate accidentally kicked over a pail of boiling water, resting on the coals. Most of it spilled on Clark's feet, and before they could get his socks off he was badly burned. He will probably be laid up for a month in the hospital.

1. "Kelly's Corner" or "Strafen's Bend," on the Esnes road. *Mort Homme* (Dead Man's Hill) and the first line German trenches are visible in the distance. A volley of shells can be seen exploding in the field to the right, Edward Kelly was killed just a few yards from here in August, 1916.
2. The rear of the *château* at Esnes. Each new Boche shell piles a little more refuse upon the *abri*, and thus makes the post below all the safer.

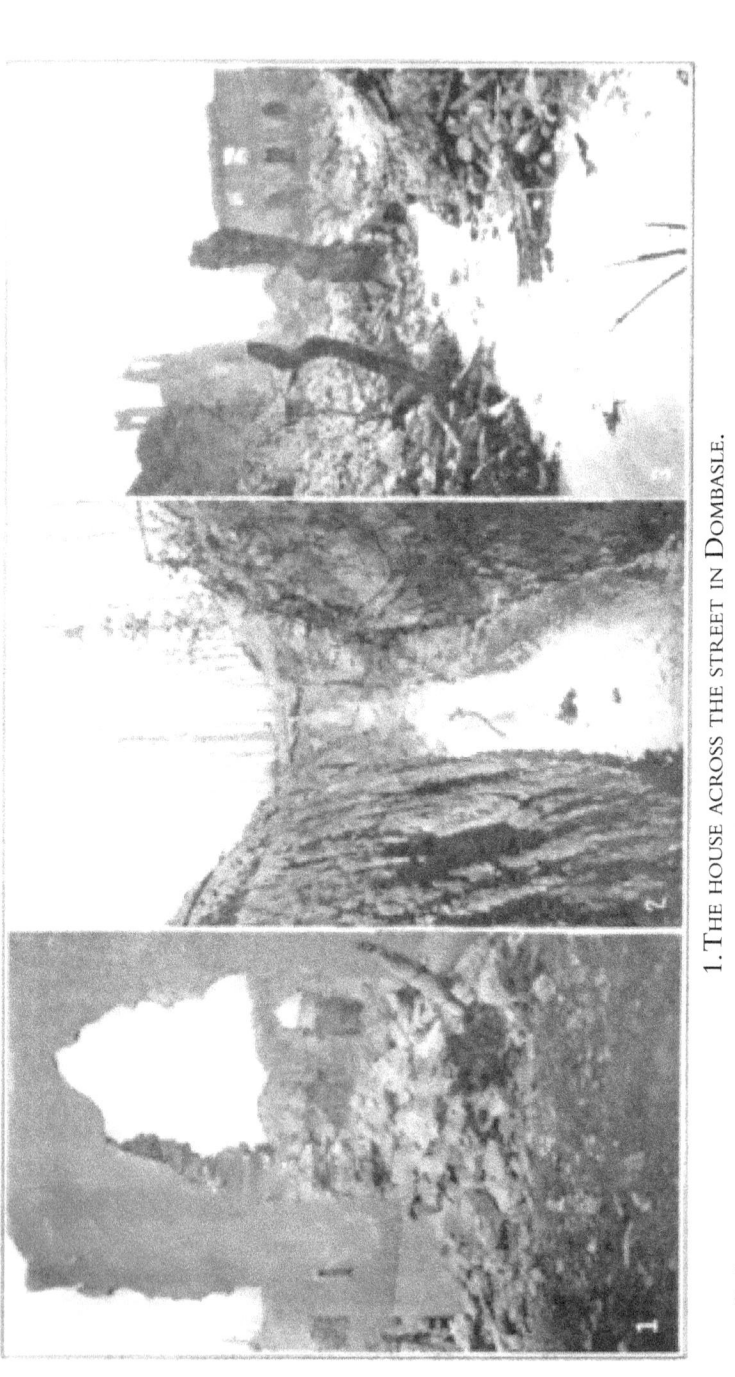

1. THE HOUSE ACROSS THE STREET IN DOMBASLE.
2. A TYPICAL COMMUNICATION TRENCH IN MARCH. THE WATER IS NOT DEEP HERE AS IT IS IN THE FIRST LINE TRENCHES. IT IS ONLY EIGHTEEN INCHES. THE POILUS USE THE LOG IN THE FOREGROUND AS A BRIDGE.
3. THE BROOK BEHIND THE CHURCH WHICH RUNS THROUGH THE "BOCHELAND."

*March 20th.* In the *abri* of the Paste de Secours at Esnes. A little afternoon on Sunday the heaviest bombardment we have yet heard started from our nearby batteries. Everyone of them from the *soixante-quinze* to the "380's" banged away for all it was worth and until midnight there was scarcely a second's interval between the shells. This was the *tir de barrage*, the preliminary to a big attack which we first thought was French but which afterwards turned out to be Boche against Hill 304 and *Mort Homme*. This naturally meant a lot of work for us and in the middle of the afternoon six or seven cars were called out and all the others were made ready to leave. (Four is the usual number sent out for our twenty-four hour stretches, three at their posts and one on call.)

My own turn came at eleven o'clock when the work was getting heavier. They gave me the Esnes run, the one I had made with Craig and where I am now, waiting until a full load of *blessés* arrive. Of course we could use no lights and as the road was constantly being shelled I felt rather nervous. We had been somewhat worked up that afternoon when Craig came in from Post Two, having seen ten men shot to pieces just one hundred yards in front of him in the Bois d'Avocourt; and Haven turned up a little later with a tale of a similar happening in another place. Furthermore, there had been a big gas attack earlier in the afternoon and four or five of the fellows had been compelled to wear their masks.

With these pleasant little stories to cheer me, I left our cantonment. I could not see the road, only an undefined streak a shade lighter than the surroundings, and I drove very slowly at first and blew my whistle at every dark spot on the horizon. Sometimes these turned out to be trees but more often they were wagons bearing ammunition and supplies to the communicating trenches from which they are carried forward either by men or *burros*. It was very hard to see them and I had many close calls not only from collision but also from breaking my rear axle in the fresh shell holes between Montzèville and Esnes. I stopped for a moment at the former post and found McLane there. He had run into a huge log, obstructing the road between the two posts and had come back here to get help. Word had been sent to Crowhurst the mechanic who came out in Houston's car. He arrived just after I did and as we were entering the *abri*, a shrapnel broke overhead and threw mud and *éclat* down the doorway.

Eight or ten more shells fell in the town while I was there and since they seemed to be after the convoys of ammunition caissons which flew by on a gallop I also kept up a pretty good speed until I was out of the place. When I passed McLane's car there was a shrapnel hole in the cowl and a piece of *éclat* in the radiator. Logs were scattered all along the road and the shell-holes became more and more numerous. I managed to get to the *château* finally and found three *grands blessés* waiting for me outside. I drove very slowly and carefully on my return trip, but sometimes I struck a bad hole which I hadn't seen and the poor fellows moaned and shrieked pathetically. I managed to get them into Dombasle finally. Here I found there was no one to relay them on to the hospital at Ville and that I would have to take them myself. So I continued on through Brocourt and Jubécourt to the H. O. E. at Ville where I left my wounded. Then I went back to Esnes again for more and kept on working until four o'clock the next afternoon. I didn't sleep for thirty-five hours and some of the men, those who had been on duty before, went four or five hours more than this.

There were a lot of fresh shell holes just outside of Esnes on one of my trips the next afternoon. I certainly prayed as I passed them with my load of *couchés* that God would help me back safely, at least to bring my car back without disaster. And I am sure my prayer was answered, for five of our cars were broken down that night and four the next, some of them rather seriously. Two machines ran into ammunition wagons and four collided in the woods. There were also several minor accidents such as running head on into a stone-wall or having a rear-wheel drop off. Of course, this seems like a good many, but I really think we were fortunate in not having any more trouble than we did. You can't expect to come out untouched on roads like these which make the worst stretch at home seem like the Lincoln highway, and with fifteen cars out at once, the majority of them driven by inexperienced drivers. Furthermore, the night was pitch-black and much of the way lay through thick woods. Then there were the lovely star-shells which come up every minute or so and after lighting up the whole landscape for eight or ten seconds, die out and leave you half-blinded by the glare.

The result of our two days' work, ending Tuesday night, was three hundred and seventy-seven wounded, carried a total distance of ten thousand kilometres. Both sides suffered severely but very little ground changed hands; and when the whole affair was over the first line trenches were nothing except a mass of shell-holes, and in many places only fifteen feet apart.

I have finally seen what I came over for, and a lot more besides war, real war, stripped of glory. For what chance has a man against a shell? And how does the awful suffering of trench life compare with the thrilling battles of the Revolution. I don't mean that it doesn't take ten times the nerve and the endurance, but there's the rub, for we have become machines, not men. I know God will protect us over here, but you realize how absolutely weak and helpless you are when a load of dead are brought in, some with arms and legs gone, others with heads and trunks mixed together; and quite often you learn there wasn't anything left to bring.

This matter of being under shellfire for the first time and of trying to drive back in the dark from Esnes, gives one a queer feeling. Payne told me on the boat coming over that he wasn't a Christian and that he didn't believe in prayer. But he said to me yesterday that he had prayed for the first time in his life out there on the Esnes road. Just as he was rounding "Kelly's Corner," a "77" landed in the road in front of him. Then two more shells came, one in the field to his right and the other a few yards behind him. "Why, Doolie," he said afterwards, "there wasn't anything else to do except to pray. I felt so little, so absolutely helpless, that I had to ask God for help. I got it too. That fourth shell didn't explode."

*March 24th.* Dombasle once again.
I crawled into my blankets here at three o'clock this morning. They sent me out about ten last evening on a special call to Post Two. I had three runs down to Ville with some *blessés* from a German *coup de main* and this kept me going for some time. Fortunately there was a full moon or I would have had a terrible time in the woods.

I had just enough pep to get up for breakfast and then was sorry that I did afterwards. It was pouring in torrents outside and the old dining-room leaked like a sieve. There was nothing to do but put on our raincoats, and stand there in that deluge, trying to swallow a plate of half-cooked oatmeal. I am afraid that our meals will be below par for a few days. André, the cook, lucky fellow, has gone to Paris on his permission and one of the truck drivers has taken his place. His first meal wasn't much of a success.

At last Section *Douze* has a mascot. Henny Houston stopped at Jubécourt today on his way back from Ville and got a little mongrel pup from his old friend Abigal in the *epicerie* there. It was baptised after lunch with the name of "Montzèville." Such a cute name for a dog.

Cooky calls our habitation on Dombasle alley the "Den of Thieves" and he certainly is right. One would think we had been brought up along with Bill Sykes in Fagin's den. Our development into kleptomaniacs began when Ott Kann hid underneath his bed about fifty pounds of time fuses and unexploded hand grenades which he had picked up near Esnes. We found out about it the same day the poor *brancardier* was killed, fooling with a grenade at Montzèville and it made us sort of nervous to see Ott sitting on his stretcher evenings banging away on his dainty little souvenirs with hammer and chisel. He appeared quite unconcerned but we weren't. The first time he tried it, the grating sound of the steel upon the brass and iron and the thought of what might happen if he struck a cap, caused us to implore him to stop.

Finally, since Ott was immovable, we all turned in, hoping that, if the thing did explode, we would miss most of the fragments because we were lying down. Ott went to Post Two on the following day, and before he returned, his relics were resting comfortably at the bottom of a neighbouring well. He immediately suspected Bradley, who was really innocent of the trick, and hid two of his three blankets just as the latter was starting for Esnes, on twenty-four hour duty. Bradley almost froze that night at the *château*, and planned vengeance upon his return. Supposing Barney to be the guilty party, from something that he had heard Ott say, he stole his shoes and a dozen packages of cigarettes which Barney had borrowed from Ott's suitcase the day before.

Of course, this complicated matters and not even our stretchers were safe after this. My mirror, my sewing kit, and all my toilet articles disappeared one by one, only to reappear a few days later on Cookies shelf or tucked away among Ott's blankets. Strange to say, it wasn't all loss. Several times I have gone to bed with three blankets over me and found five there in the morning. And not a soul in the room would know anything about it. If Crowhurst makes a little paper cutter out of a compression band or perhaps a salt and pepper shaker from a Boche machine-gun bullet, and we feel that it would mean more to us than it would to him, we persuade ourselves that it is really ours and get possession of it at the first opportunity. We thought at first this kleptomania was confined to our own room; but it has spread throughout the section, even to the plutocrats across the street. Stealing has become almost a virtue, as it was with the Spartans: you are a wonder if you can get away with it. But whatever happens, don't get caught.

Barney Faith and I laid in a supply of wood this afternoon which ought to last us a month. But it is still pretty cold and Bradley and Cook keep the fireplace so well filled up that we have to have two or three cords on hand all the time. We keep it stacked up in the corner where the piano used to be. The two of us ran my ambulance down the street to the wreck of an old mansion, filled the back chuck full of banister pickets, assorted furniture and wainscoting which we tore from the walls, and carried it back to our one room apartment on the hill.

It is twenty minutes to ten and we are still sitting around the fire. Crow pulled out his mouth-organ a little while again and is playing every ragtime he can think of. Cook has just received a long expected cheque from home and is so happy about it that he is practising a clog dance on Ott Kann's bed. Ott is on duty at Post Three.

*March 26th.*            Esnes The Winecellar of the old *château*.

I stumbled into the morgue last night when I was trying to locate one of the *brancardiers*, out behind the *château*. It had been clear all evening and a beautiful moon was rising above the hill towards Montzèville. But its rays were not beautiful within the morgue. They showed far too clearly the mangled limbs and bodies of a dozen Frenchmen who had been brought down from *Mort Homme* the night before. Here a rough gunny sack covered the decapitated trunk of a young machine-gunner; and alongside it lay the abdomen and legs of another poor *poilu* whose feet had already rotted away before a kind Boche shell put him out of misery. Bouvier told me several of them had been stuck in the mud out there for three days after the attack and although unwounded when shells were breaking all around them they had died of hunger and exposure. People at home think that we are making tremendous sacrifices to come over here and do this work. But they are nothing compared to those which the simple, uneducated *poilu* makes.

When I was little, I used to spend hours over stories of wars in Egypt and France, in England and Russia. And I have thought since then how little truth there was in any of them; the fact that the war had been fought often being the only reasonably true statement. The *poilus* have started on the same plan; and I presume in ten years a number of books on exaggerated myths of the present war will be on sale. Nevertheless, their tales are interesting, and usually very exciting. We were all gathered in the *abri* at the post in Esnes last night, seven *brancardiers* and LeFevre and myself, when one of them sprung this

### Brass Time Fuse from a German "77" (3-inch Shell)

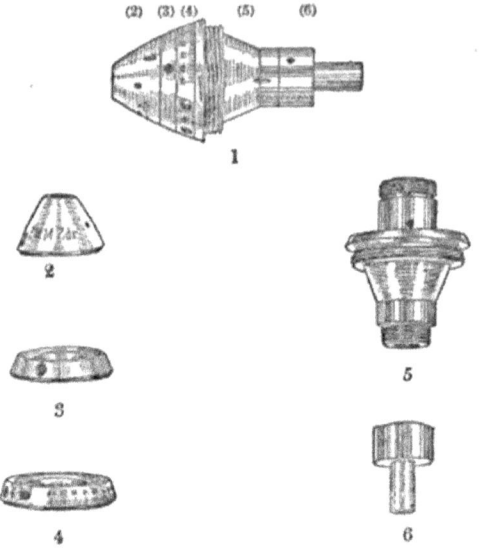

1. The time fuse assembled, ready to be screwed on to the shell proper.

2. The top of the fuse which contains the spring and fulminate of mercury cap. The latter explodes from iner- tia on leaving the gun.

3. First ring, with groove filled with powder which burns until it comes to hole in (4). It is ignited by the explosion of the cap in (2).

4. Second ring, also filled with powder, which is ignited from (3) and which burns as far as the unit indicated on ring. This ring is set for the second at which it is desired that the shell shall explode over the enemy's lines.

5. Base of time fuse. Upper part contains trigger and lower part tube through which the flame passes which explodes the shell itself.

6. The covering over last part of passage.

1. THE ANTI-AIRCRAFT "75." ON THE HILL IN STE. MENEHOULD. THE AUDI-PHONE CONSISTS OF A PHONOGRAPH HORN, A LONG HOSE, AND A SET OF TIGHTLY STRUNG WIRES. WITH THIS APPARATUS AN ENEMY AEROPLANE MOTOR CAN BE HEARD TEN MILES AWAY.
2. STE. MENEHOULD SCHOOLBOYS, WATCHING THE GUN ABOVE SHELLING A GERMAN PLANE 12,000 FEET ABOVE THE CITY.
3. OUR APARTMENTS IN STE. MENEHOULD. THE STRETCHER WITH ITS REGULATION IRON NECK AND ANKLE REST IS COVERED WITH BLANKETS FULL OF LITTLE THINGS THE FOUR BASINS ARE USED FOR DEVELOPING PICTURES.

1. Children scrambling for little American flags, which we are tossing down to them from the barn window.
2. Young Monsieur Deliege and his sister Suzanne. He is wearing his dress suit for he has just taken his first communion.
3. A section of a hospital train. Each compartment holds four stretcher cases.

story. He called it, "How the Crown Prince came to Esnes," and he says the affair occurred early in 1915 when the war was still young and crossing the lines was not so difficult as it is now. It happened that the Boches were hammering away at Verdun as usual and were planning their big Spring offensive.

If they could get all of Hill 304 and *Mort Homme*, besides Forts Douaumont and Vaux the game would almost be up for the French on the entire salient. So one dark night in February, the Crown Prince, who wasn't quite sure what forces the French had in this sector, decided to dash across himself in his staff car, shoot down over the hill into Esnes and get some information from one of the general's staff, a major in the French Army, who was of course a spy. The old road from Montfaucon to Esnes was pretty badly torn by shell-fire at that time, but there wasn't a single trench cut through it. They were all burrowed under it. And as for barb-wire, they weren't using any yet on the hill. The prince and two of his intimate friends, dressed in French officers' uniforms and driving a "Baby Peugeot," of Parisian manufacture, crossed the lines in a drizzling rain about midnight after a scouting party had given the "*sehr gut*" signal. They bounced from one shell crater to another down the narrow, winding road into the village.

But they got to the *château* all right, where the headquarters were then. The three men entered the *château*, conferred with the major in his private *abri* and afterwards joked and drank healths with the other officers in the main apartment. But they stayed a trifle too long. The wine had its effect and the Crown Prince began to get a little careless with his French. But only one man had noticed it, for all the others were "happy," too. This was the sergeant on guard at the door. He tried to whisper in the commandant's ear but the old fellow pushed him away; and the colonel wouldn't even look at him. Suddenly the major entered, said that a message had come for the guests and would they please step outside for a moment.

This was the last that was ever seen of them at Esnes. But they know that the car carried four men back to Germany instead of the three which it brought over. And the sergeant was court-martialled for not telling the colonel before it was too late.

*March 28th,* 1917.                                   Dombasle-en-Argonne,

It is a few minutes before midnight. I have just returned from my twenty-four hours, which stretched into thirty this time, at Montzèville and Esnes. I dropped asleep last evening in the *abri* at the former place and when I awoke early this morning I found myself lying fully dressed on a pile of straw with no blankets over me. Naturally I hadn't slept very well, but I felt I had been lucky not to have been called out at two or three o'clock. At seven I went over to the *Poste de Secours abri* and had breakfast with the *brancardiers*. They are the same men who were here last week except that there is one missing. Jean Picot, I think his name was, had his hand blown off recently by a grenade which he was trying to unload. He was evacuated to Ville sur Couzances but the chances for his recovery are very slight. Monsieur Guerin, the dapper little adjutant, is still here. As usual, he talked to me in English and I answered each time in French. He is quite serious about it, and corrects all of my mistakes very carefully.

Across the street from us was one of the army telephone exchanges. I watched them for some time this morning as they were trying to connect "Dead Man's Hill," Dugout Number Twenty-seven, with a busy colonel's quarters in the Bois de Bethelainville. I couldn't make a great deal out of the conversation, so I soon left them and went into their kitchen. A middle-aged man with a rough, black beard stood beside the stove which happened to be one of the regulation army kitchen wagons placed in one corner of the room. I shouted "*Bon jour, Monsieur*," at him two or three times before he heard me. Finally he turned around and looked me over very carefully. Then (I think someone must have told him that an American section was nearby) he burst out with, "Well I'll be darned. You are the first person from the States I have seen for eighteen months. What's your home town, anyway."

He said it all so fast that I could not make him out for a minute. But I came to shortly and then it was my turn to ask questions. He told me that he had gone to America when he was seventeen, and settled in New York City. For some years, along with another Frenchman, he had conducted a well-known hair-dressing establishment on Fifth Avenue. When the war broke out he had debated for some time whether he ought to leave his family or not. But finally he couldn't stand it any longer; and so it happened that he sailed back to France in the fall of 1914. We got into a long conversation; he wanted to know all about America and what had happened there lately, and I was trying to find out more about him. Then in order to cement our friendship he offered me a cup of coffee flavoured with a spoonful of their terrible *cognac*. It took a long time to get it down for it choked me if I swallowed much at once. But excepting his love for *cognac*, and *eau de vie*, he was a fine chap. I promised to look him up the next time I came to Montzèville.

At four o'clock I rode up to Esnes with only an occasional shell dropping near; but the French were peppering *Mort Homme* and I hurried along in order to get to the *château* before the Boche began to reply. Fifteen or twenty shells dropped around the post a few minutes after I arrived but I was in the *abri* by that time.

Chauvenet has just come in from Post Two. On his way out a "210" landed in the middle of the road just in front of his car and a great piece of steel tore through the top of his car not ten inches from his head, and dropped into the back of the ambulance. He did not know that the car had been touched until half an hour later, for he was so stunned by the force of the explosion and so overcome by the gases of the shell through which he was forced to ride that he barely got out alive. Everyone is envious and wishes that it had happened to him—at least they say so.

I picked up a chap near Brocourt today who was on his way back to *Mort Homme* after his permission. He had walked all the way from Bar-le-Duc that day and was all tired out. He was mighty glad to get the ride for he had orders to be back in his company before midnight. We talked for a while in jerky little sentences; I, using the usual "*n'est ce pas*" and "*Comprenez—vous*" and he always relying on "*C'est la Guerre*" for an answer to my questions. At one place we passed a flock of strange birds. I pointed to them and mumbled something to signify that I wanted to know what they were. He simply said "*oiseau*" and I replied as well as I could that we didn't have any *oiseaus* in America. He looked rather surprised and muttered something about having always heard that *Etats Unis* was a queer sort of a place. I discovered when I got back to the cantonment that the word *oiseau* means bird.

Cook relieved me at nine o'clock, saying that three big "boys" had fallen near him as he passed through Montzèville. This was a pleasant send off and I pictured a delightful little journey back to Dombasle. But the stars were out when I started and a sprinkling of snow upon the ground made it very easy to keep on the road. I had only one *blessé*, for things were quiet in the trenches today.

*March 30.*                                                                         Dombasle again.

Harry came in at four this morning and got Crowhurst and me out of bed. Haven's car had broken down near Esnes and we were to go out in 464 to fix it. Coan went along with us. We found it straddling an old stone wall not far from the post. He had wandered off the road and run square into it when a star shell went out and left him in total darkness. The front axle was badly bent and the triangle rod was almost tied in a knot. Of course we couldn't straighten the axle but we put in a new rod in the dark and managed to tow the car home. The *blessés* with which he had started out had in the meanwhile been transferred to another car and taken to Ville.

Thursday night the *blessés* from the morning attack began to pile in at Esnes. I went on at eight o'clock as a reserve. The first time down I had one *couché* who couldn't stand the pain. He almost drove me crazy with his shrieking and yells of "For God's Sake, Stop." And several times when I happened to hit a shell hole or a log accidentally, he actually rose up in his agony and pounded with his bare fists upon the wall of the ambulance. But I knew that I couldn't help him by stopping, and I felt that I might save his life if I hurried. After I got out of Montzèville, he quieted down and I supposed this was because the road was so much smoother.

But not until I stopped in front of the hospital at Ville did I learn the truth. The poor fellow had died on the road. Soon after this Haven and Allen collided in the Bethelainville Woods. I took Jim out in my car to get them in. I left him here with Haven to work on the cars and went on by myself to Esnes. It was certainly an awful night, dark as pitch and a sleety rain blowing into my eyes. However, I got through by God's help, passing Dunham's car which was laid up with a broken rear axle just outside the woods. I waited two hours at the post for *couchés*, Tenney and Houston leaving with their loads before me. Some sad cases were brought in while we were waiting. One fellow, with his foot almost severed at the ankle, lay there without a whimper while they amputated it. Another man with his head caved in like an old cantaloupe, lay beside him. He looked hopeless but the doctors bandaged him and sent him to Ville.

I was doing my best to dodge a couple of shell holes near Strafen's corner (one of the spots the Boches love to pepper) on my last trip tonight when I overtook a poor courier, walking, and pushing his bicycle beside him through the mud. We drivers are not supposed to carry any soldiers and this wasn't an ideal place to stop. But the poor fellow was dead tired and I knew if he felt worse than I did he'd be mighty thankful for a lift. So I pulled on my emergency and yelled to him to throw his bike over the hood and jump in himself if he wanted a ride down to Dombasle. . . . I left him saying "*Merci, Monsieur, Merci*" outside of the village just at sunrise and went on to Ville with my *blessés*. I got back to the cantonment at 6 130, having had no rest for more than thirty hours and getting something like five hours sleep in the last fifty. Two of the men had been on duty at Post Two before, and worked for more than forty hours without sleep.

A wonderful surprise came today, a box from home. Besides a lot of food which included twenty packages of chewing gum, some crackers and a two pound box of chocolates which disappeared like *brancardiers* when a shell whistles, there were a dozen magazines, a pair of shoes, a compass which I will probably use more in Paris than out here, and some good photographic paper which I can't get in France. The crackers lasted five minutes, the candy until supper time, and I have one package of gum left. But no matter how fast the stuff disappeared, it was certainly great fun getting it.

*March 31.* Dombasle

While I was snoozing comfortably in my car today, Gilmore started the motor and had driven out of the cantonment before I realized what he was doing. I think he wanted to prove to me that a *couché* has no easy ride in one of our ambulances, for he went over kerbstones and rock-piles and into ditches and shell holes, like those which we run into on the Esnes road. The jar was terrific. Sometimes it shook my body all over; and again when we hit a sharp bump, like the kerb, my feet, along with the whole rear end of the stretcher, were thrown twelve inches into the air and then fell with a crash onto the floor of the car.

I wonder what the girls back home would think of the love-letter reading contest we had in our room tonight. There were four of us there, Eaton, Payne, Frazer and I, sitting around the fire and having a terrible debate over whether or not the Boston *Post* had the second largest morning circulation in the country. Eaton swore that it had, because he had worked on it for a month about five years ago. He rashly offered ten to one odds, and all three of us took him up at fifty *francs* apiece. We intended to prove it by my *Almanac* which the family notified me recently had been sent by parcel post. Then the conversation switched to girls and old Payne claimed he had the most devoted one in all California. Frazer began boasting about his, and before we knew it, they were pulling out their respective letters and each was trying to prove that his was far more in love with him than the other. Eaton and I were to act as judges.

Payne's turned out to be a nice, sensible girl who had just had the measles, and said "Dear Mart," and "Oh I wish you were here," and "As ever yours, Dinah." ... Frazer's was a bright little thing, very peppy and with lots of interesting things to say. But she didn't rant much about her love, and couldn't have used the word "Dear" more than three or four times in the body of the letter. Eaton wouldn't wait long enough to hand out a decision after this. He pulled open one of his own and it beat the other two all hollow. His beloved began with "Dearest, darling, honeybunchingest, lovey-dovey Robinson," and filled up the whole affair with such absolute nonsense on how she couldn't stand his absence another minute and how she wanted to fly to him, that we were shrieking with laughter before he had read five lines. He got the prize which happened to be a forty pound pot of lead melted from shrapnel balls. He can lug it back to America if he wishes.

*April Fool's Day.*            Midnight in the *abri* at Post Two

I was sent out here exactly nineteen hours ago to find Ray Eaton. He had gone to Post Three two hours before that, on a special call and hadn't been heard of since he left there with a load of *couchés*. Now Bois d'Avocourt is divided into innumerable little squares by dozens of military roads which lead from battery to battery and from one cantonment to another. Some of them are in a frightful condition and we figured that Ray had strayed into one of these and gotten stuck. It was just by chance that I found him. I came to a crossroads, turned to the right when I should have kept straight ahead and discovered his car at the foot of a steep hill. He explained what had happened in a few words. His clutch had given out completely when he started up the hill and after backing down to the bottom in neutral, he found his reverse wouldn't pull at all. And furthermore it would have been extremely difficult to have turned around in the dark upon this muddy, narrow road, especially with the load of *blessés* which he had.

Several times during his long wait he had walked back to the main road, thinking one of the other cars might be passing; but none had come and of course he did not dare to leave his wounded alone for any length of time. I managed to get 464 back to back with his machine and together we changed the *couchés*. The lower two were easy enough but it took every ounce of our strength to lift the third *blessé* up to the top rack of the ambulance. After I had closed the back I watched Coan as he tried to climb the hill. Minus the heavy burden he succeeded in making the ascent and a minute later disappeared over the crest. After running down to Ville with my load I came back to Post Three and then on to Two.

By this time it was six o'clock, so late that I didn't lie down at all. I put a couple of sticks on the fire and dozed on a stool in front of it until the *brancardiers* awakened and started their breakfast of bread and coffee. While we were eating I read a letter which came yesterday from Tony Cucuron, the young artilleryman whom I met in Brillon six weeks ago. He had promised then to write to me in English, because he thought it would be easier for me to read. I am quoting it below for I think it expresses very clearly the feelings of a boy, sick and tired of the war. Of course he has made a number of mistakes in grammar but considering the short time he studied English he did remarkably well. Here it is:

The Thirteenth of March,
Dear sir and friend, The French Front
I am sure you wil forget me for not writing for some week. Here as you know we are never free.
It is too difficult and besides we are so tired that we have no courage to write. Now, I am on the front and our guns are not far from the German's trenches. I should not tell you news about my life for you know what it is. Our life, it is sad and dull, and we are awaiting for the end of the war. I am some little happy for I hope and think the day is at hand. It is too the opinion of the whole part. I longe anxiously to return home, my heart aches to be far from my native town.
It is a very sweet country with a blue and sunny sky. After the war I will return home and then end my studies at the "*Université de Droit*" of Toulouse. I do not know what your feelings are about what I am saying, but I suppose you also are in a hurry to return home or for the less to see the war over.
Perhaps you wish to go to England or to settle in France. I like very, very our brotherland and after the war I wil spend three or six months in London. My dear friend, you see that I keep my promises I have written. Please write often it is the sincere desire of yours very truly,

TONY CUCURON

During the forenoon I waited around outside the *abri* and since no *blessés* seemed to be forthcoming, I strolled over to an observation tree several hundred yards distant. It was a big beech, more than sixty feet high, and appeared to have a small screened platform in the topmost branches. When I had climbed up about thirty steps I came to a place where a shell had torn away half of the trunk; but it seemed solid enough so I took a chance and went on to the top. From here I could see for miles over the front, beginning with *Mort Homme* on the right, then across Hill 304, Avocourt, and the surrounding forest and ending with the plateau above Vauquois. It was wonderfully interesting to me to watch the crude, zigzag lines twisting in and out among the hills and valleys. I was only sorry that I hadn't a pair of field glasses along. They would have made it easier to see the trenches and some of the "150's" bursting in the valley beyond me would also have shown up more clearly.

McLane who had been spending the night at Post Three, got a bogus telephone message to come up here for a wounded officer and dropped in about noon. Not a *blessé* had arrived for hours so we talked for a while and finally started to dig for *fusées* and compression bands in the fresh shell holes behind the post. There was one only a few hours old in which we were particularly interested. We hadn't begun to dig before we discovered that a "gas" shell had fallen here. And it was tear gas at that. Water literally rolled from our eyes and this was soon followed by an awful choking sensation. We put on our gas masks immediately and from then on, until we found the base of the shell, buried several feet underground, we didn't remove the masks at all. We had to work very slowly, for the air is filtered through in such small quantities, that you can't breathe as you normally do when working.

Note. A month later: I carried the steel base, half full of clay, back to Dombasle, and during all the weeks we stayed here it never lost its gassy odour.

A couple of *poilus* and I had a grand time trying to say a few simple things to one another tonight. We sat before the fire in the damp *abri* where I am now writing and where the smoke hangs down from the ceiling in a cloud two feet thick. (You have to crawl on your hands and knees when you move about in the room.) While I was getting in deep over some complicated idea which I wanted to impart to them, and was gesticulating wildly to explain it, a *brancardier* tapped me lightly on the shoulder and said—"*Encore des Blessés, Monsieur.*" I reluctantly put on my heavy canvas mackinaw and went out into the night. The *brancardiers* had already shoved the stretchers into the car and closed up the back when I arrived. I filled my radiator as usual from my reserve can, (it is still so cold that we are obliged to drain the

1. The gasoline locomotive and train of the narrow-gauge railway which carry shells and supplies up to the lines.
2. Brancardiers putting a couché (stretcher case) in the ambulance at St. Thomas.
3. "464" and her driver. Directly above the hood, on the wall behind, is posted President Wilson's message of April 17th, 1917.

1. Three poilus in a front line trench near St. Thomas.
2. A first line communication trench above St. Thomas. The French have barbed-wire stretched overhead to prevent entrance here by the enemy.

water every time we stop the motor for more than a minute or so), gave her one twist and started off for Ville.

It was frightfully dark in the woods and every now and then I stopped my car, got out and looked about to see if I were still on the road. At the first crossroads I almost ran down a four horse artillery caisson; after that I kept my little tin whistle going pretty steadily, and fully half a dozen times a shrill return came back out of the night when I saw nothing at all. But at the fork near Post Four my luck failed me. Instead of bearing to the left to go to Dombasle, I missed the turn entirely and headed in the other direction. When I discovered my error it was too late to go back. I had never been over the road that I was now on, and it was darker than ever. I could only see a few feet beyond the radiator cap. But I remembered from my map that it led to Recicourt; and I knew that from there on to Dombasle I could go on the main Verdun-Sainte Menehould highway. I drove very slowly, at times not more than four miles an hour, until I was safely down the long hill leading into the village. There wasn't a truck, not even a *ravitaillement* cart on the highway and I speeded up to fifteen miles an hour.

I got to Dombasle without any more trouble, stopped for a second at the Doctor's office to tell the man on call to take my place at Post Two, and set off again for Ville. My eyes were very tired from the strain of constantly peering through the darkness and so when I came to the "*Eteignez les lumieres blanches*" sign on the hill outside of Brocourt (this town is about ten miles from the first lines, and about as close as lights can be used safely) I stopped a minute to throw on my head-lights. But in doing so I took all the pressure off the footbrake and a few seconds later, when I turned on the switch and the lights illuminated the road ahead, I found the whole car going rapidly backwards down the hill. I jammed on the emergency brake and all three foot pedals and the car came to an abrupt halt a few feet farther down. I got out of my seat to see where I was, and discovered that the rear wheels of the machine were at the top of a steep bank over which we would have tumbled if we had gone six inches further. I made a silent prayer as we started up the hill, thanking God for saving us from disaster.

At Ville I put the patients into the hands of a couple of attendants who carried them into a large waiting room and after examining the tickets pinned to each of their coats, which gave the nature of the injury, they carried the poor fellows off to their respective wards.

Then I went out into the night again and turned old 464 towards

Post Two. It was a great treat riding with my headlights on full blast and I hated to turn them off again at Brocourt. It became very difficult driving after this, and I was almost sorry that I had used my lights at all, for my eyes had grown accustomed to the glare and it was fully five minutes before I could see the road at all. I got along all right for a mile or so after this, but when I neared the long hill leading down into the village of Dombasle, my sight failed me completely. The car seemed to be hitting an endless series of great "thank you mam's" which shot the front wheels high up in the air and brought them down with a terrific crash onto the stony road.

To save my life, I couldn't see what the trouble was or what the obstacles blocking the road were. I went pounding on down the hill, hanging on to the wheel for dear life as I bounced from one of these awful things to another. And finally, when a speck of moon peeped out from behind a cloud, I saw what was causing the trouble. There, spread out carefully on each side of the road, at intervals of perhaps twenty-five feet, were piles of crushed rock, ten or twelve inches high, which the repairers had dumped there. I had been trying to straddle these as I came down and would have soon run smack into the bank if my old friend, the moon, hadn't appeared.

I am back again at Post Two now, safe and sound. But it is no longer midnight as I headed the first page of today's diary. My watch tells me that I have been writing for two hours. I had intended to go to bed after I had finished this but my good friend Angeron, the *brancardier*, says no. There are *Encore des Blessés* outside.

*April 5,* 1917. Post Two again.

It is eight-thirty, an hour past the regular time for the relief man to show up, and still no one has come. We no longer change shifts at four in the afternoon, as we used to when we first went to Esnes. The Boches have been deliberately firing on our ambulances lately, and we now change runs in the dark, in order to avoid any unnecessary driving in daylight. Most of us would really rather take the run in daytime, for with all due respect to German shells, it is no fun going over the old road in the dark.

I brought my own blanket roll, hoping to have a quiet sleep, but they brought in "frozen feet" all night long and I had to carry them back to Ville. I made seven runs altogether and carried thirty *blessés*. If I remember rightly, only four of them were *couchés*. All the remainder had that awful disease "*Pied gélé*" where the foot slowly rots away, and leaves the bone bare.

I sat in a shell hole outside of the *abri* for a while this afternoon, watching the Boches pepper one of our "150" batteries about two hundred yards behind me. They shelled it for over an hour, and I had a grand time listening to each projectile as it whistled over my head, and broke a few seconds later in the woods beyond. I discovered, as it grew darker and I could see the flash of the exploding shell, that the noise from this took several seconds to come to me, after the explosion. And more than that, I noticed that the whistle continued for a short length of time after the shell had actually exploded. Therefore I naturally concluded from this that the nearer you were to an exploding projectile, the shorter would be the whistle: and that it would be impossible to hear at all the approach of a very close shell.

At supper tonight the good news came, which we, and especially the Frenchmen, have been waiting to hear for months—"*Les Etats Unis ont declaré la guerre contre l'Allemagne.*" One of the *brancardiers* returning from his furlough in Paris, broke the news to us. We were all below in the *abri*, making a great uproar over "*soupe*" (a *poilu* can make more noise over a plate of hot soup than any other human being) when he came rushing down the muddy stairs and shouted to us what had happened. *Soupe* was forgotten for the moment, as we plied him with questions and pored over the copies of "*Le Parisien*" and "*Le Matin*" which he gave to us. So America was really in the war; President Wilson had made a great speech in Congress and denounced Germany; no longer would France regard her chances of final victory as slim. And each one of those simple *poilus* wrung my hand, and asked me if I didn't think we would have our troops here soon.

I don't believe I was ever prouder of America than at that moment; and as they pointed to a faded old banner, hanging from their smoke-blackened ceiling, in which one could barely distinguish the colours, and I showed them the little American flag, pinned to my coat we realized that the "*Bleu, blanc et rouge*" and the "Red, White, and Blue," were one and the same thing.

We talked together, or rather tried to talk, for a long time after the meal was over; finally I went outdoors, for I thought Cooky, or whoever was to relieve me, might be here already. And as I walked through the trees, I thought of many things, of Europe when the war would be over, of home, and if I would ever see it again. Suddenly I stumbled, and looking down to see what had tripped me, I saw a pile of dead soldiers, mangled by shell beyond all recognition. Some had been torn in two at the waist, and of others, very little but the head and shoulders remained. But they were Frenchmen, they had given all they had for France, and they must be treated accordingly. Tomorrow morning the priest would come to get the few personal effects of each man so that he could wrap them up and send them to their respective families. Sometimes these packages were very small, containing, perhaps, only a knife, a few cigarettes, and a wallet; but I have never seen one which didn't contain the pictures of his loved ones. After this a couple of *brancardiers* will dig a rude grave nearby, the priest will say a few last words, the grave will be filled with earth, and a little wooden cross placed at the head to mark the spot.

I hear someone coming now. He has his exhaust pipe disconnected and is making a terrible fuss. It sounds like "Percy Pyne, of Princeton," (name-plate on the car) and if so, then it's Cooky, so *"assez aujourd'hui."*

*April 6.* Esnes again.

I am on duty at Esnes again and am using a few leisure moments, trying to write by candlelight in Le Fevre the chemist's cabin. It was once the vault of a deep wine-cellar, but now, with the ruins of the *château* piled upon it, it forms a very respectable *abri*.

Last night I carried two *couchés* to Ville from here, and on the way back, I stopped at Jubécourt to see if I could buy a little wine which M. Bouvier wants for mass on Easter Sunday. The main street of the village is on a steep grade. I pulled up opposite the *epicerie* and leaving the motor running, I wandered around the neighbourhood to see if I could get the "*Vin Rouge*." But when I found all the inhabitants in bed, I returned to the spot where I left the car. To my dismay it was no longer there. And looking about, endeavouring to find what had become of it, I saw several hundred yards down the hill, the indistinct form of an ambulance: I ran down to it and found it up against the stone wall of a house. I thought surely the front axle would be twisted or a wheel taken off; but luckily it had not attained any great speed on the way down, and had hit the wall rather gently. Except for the triangle being slightly bent, the car was unhurt. I suppose the vibrations of the motor running idle finally loosened the emergency brake, and since it was on a steep decline the car had started forward.

I had quite a busy night. The trip to Esnes was very slow on account of the hundreds of ammunition wagons, and companies of reserve troops which blocked the road. Finally I arrived at the post and slept for two hours before I was called out with a "*grand couché.*" I drove pretty slowly but got stuck somehow in a new shell-hole near the entrance to the *château*. I couldn't budge the machine by myself, so I had to get my *assis* out to help me. They weren't very enthusiastic about the job, since they were suffering from their wounds, but they pushed as hard as they could, while I put on the power; and after three or four trials, the flivver, climbed over the edge in fine shape. I carried the *blessés* as usual to Ville, and then returned to Montzèville. All the brancardiers were asleep here. I found a stretcher in one corner and a couple of *blessé* blankets on the straw. They were bloodstained and dirty, but in the dampness of the *abri*, much better than no covering at all. I curled up in them and managed to sleep until Craig came in at three o'clock and sent me back to Esnes. They pulled me out of bed here a few hours later, with another load.

The Boches are shelling "Strafen Corner" considerably now. Half a dozen new holes have sprung up in the road itself overnight and there are twenty or thirty more on either side. But the town itself is worse. Every night it is crowded with *burros*, troops, supplies, and ammunition caissons going in every imaginable direction. I got caught in the jam near the barbed-wire stores last night and had to wait ten minutes until the road was clear once more. I shouldn't want to be a traffic cop in this place. Six roadworkers were killed here by one shell last week, and one of the officers from the post was wounded by shrapnel yesterday.

I am down in Le Fevre's *abri*, waiting for Faith to relieve me. I hope he gets through the village all right. Six or seven volleys of four shells apiece have fallen there during the last twenty minutes. I guess there won't be so many coming when I leave, for they have been working pretty steadily. I hear Faith's whistle outside now. It means back to Dombasle and a good night's rest.

*April 7.*                                                                           Dombasle.

Chauvenet left today for Salonique; he goes on the mail truck Bar-le-Duc, then to Paris and Marseilles by railroad, and finally on a slow little Mediterranean freighter to Greece. I was sorry to see him go. I will never forget our walk together last Friday when we visited the sausage beyond Jouy and ate our meagre lunch of bread and *confiture* in the woods behind it. Later we walked to the summit of the big hill overlooking Bethelainville. We went cross country all the way, and at one place happened to wander across a lonely rifle range where a company of young soldiers were busy practising. Luckily they saw us in time, and we came out untouched.

Further on, at the top of the hill above the village, we got a marvellous view of *Mort Homme* and could make out very clearly the two lines of trenches stretching along its sides. Beyond lay the Bois de Corbeaux and at its foot the ruins of Chattancourt. To the left, miles behind, we could distinguish the towers of lofty Montfaucon. Fort Douaumont was over the hills on the right, and we could see the outskirts of Verdun which lay hidden in the valley of the Meuse. In the foreground, we could make out the French second and third line trenches, and here and there about Vigneville a *"soixante quinze"* shot out a jut of flame. The! French had a number of sausages up, and we were able to pick out two Boche balloons, far behind their own lines. There were a few shells bursting in the valley and big puffs of smoke rose regularly from *Mort Homme*. The artillery never seems to stop work here.

Gilmore and I go souvenir-hunting regularly now. We explored the old munition depot yesterday which a Boche aviator blew up last summer. There were 40,000 loaded shells, both shrapnel and high explosive, stored there, and hundreds of empty casings, fuses, and *douilles*. They all went up together because of one measly bomb. We brought home a quart of shrapnel, and a number of compression bands.

Gilmore has found the tip of a "380," (it weighs about forty pounds) and also enough parts of a "75" to construct the whole shell. Everybody seems to have gone souvenir-crazy. Not only do we bring in all sorts of junk from the posts, but we spend every minute here making *briquets*, paper knives, aluminium rings, and various do-dads from Boche bullets. Whenever anyone brings in a hand grenade or a time fuse we always take the thing apart. It's taking a terrible chance, but we seem to forget the present and look forward to our happy homes in years to come, with the relics we brought from Dombasle reposing on the mantelpiece. My best souvenir so far is an old cavalry sword I got in Jubécourt. It is over four feet long, has a wonderful edge, and dates back to 1822. I got it for a *franc* from an old man who seemed very anxious to get rid of it and all he asked was enough money to buy a bottle of cheap wine. I think some officer left it there by mistake and never returned for it. It is a fine souvenir and I hope I can get it back to America.

There is a little attack on tonight, probably in the sector west of Avocourt. I hope it won't fill up Post Two and get me out of bed

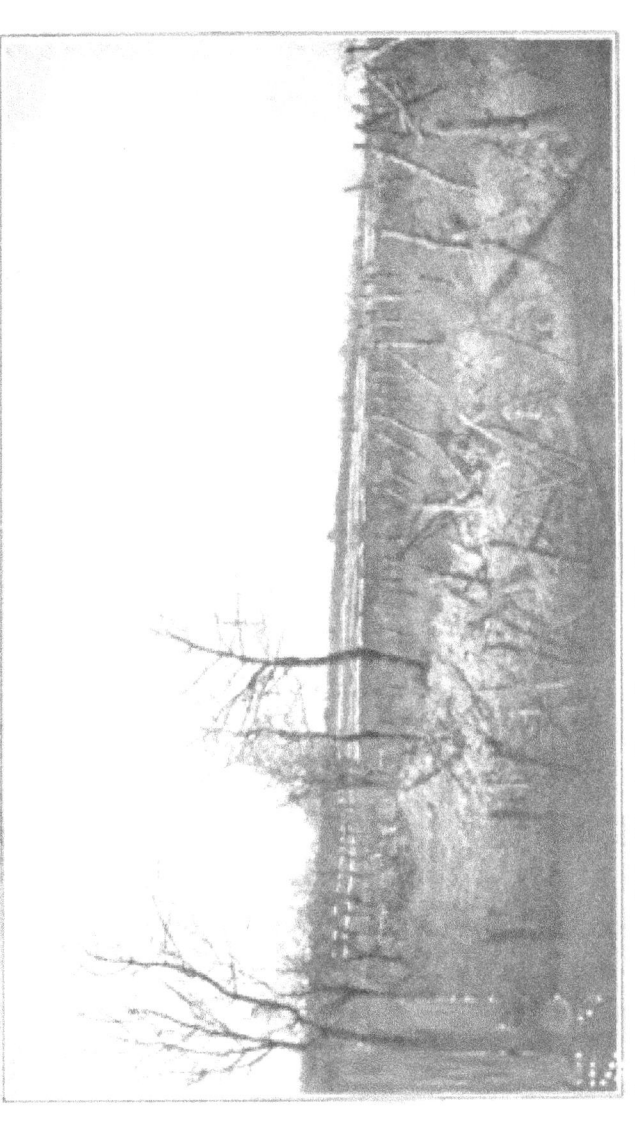

A quiet part of "No Man's Land" near St. Thomas. The ruins of Servon, a French village now in the hands of the Germans, are visible in the distance. In the foreground is the French barbed-wire, and just beyond, the Boche. Directly behind this can be seen the three lines of the enemy's trenches.

1. The: Poste de Secoures at La Harazee. This station is the closest to the Boches that we ever had. It's less than 300 yards over the hill to "No Man's Land."
2. A firing trench and hand grenade post. The sign "PP3X" is the name of the trench.
3. Two poilus, one with a sunshade, resting in a front line trench on a hot summer afternoon. It is just 100 yards to the Boches from here.

around three o'clock tomorrow morning.

Just before I started writing tonight, while I was rummaging around my suitcase for a clean pair of underclothes—(I haven't changed them since I wouldn't like to say how long)—I found, in the toe of one of my socks, an egg, which I bought for the party in Jubécourt three weeks ago and never used. Immediately I decided to fry it; I put some mahogany table legs on the fire (they make wonderful coals) and borrowed Gilmore's shell-casing dish to use as a frying pan. I had my Ford pliers for a handle. But just after I had broken the egg, I noticed that I had no lard. The kitchen was locked up securely and all the Ford axle grease was packed away in the white truck. Suddenly I remembered that I had a jar of Vaseline, which I had brought with me from America. I dug it out of my duffle-bag, rubbed it a little on the pan, dumped on the egg and put it on the fire to cook. Two minutes later I was munching the result, a crisp, savoury egg; the slight oil-refinery flavour made me homesick for Pennsylvania. But this in no way prevented me from enjoying it immensely.

*April 10th*, 1917. Dombasle

Powell came back on the mail truck today from Bar-le-Duc where he has been ever since we left Longeville, recuperating from a severe attack of pneumonia. Before we could tell him about the attacks we had been through and the all too frequent "*tir de barrage*" he burst out with "Say, fellows, you ought to have heard that big explosion from over the hills a few minutes ago. It must have been a shell going off."

Ott's love for souvenirs almost finished him this morning. It seems that some *poilu* gave him a little round iron cylinder with two little screws on the end, for a present. He brought it back to Dombasle and told us that he had been given this little thing to use as a gasoline lamp. When he took out one of the screws a queer, yellowish powder came out and he put it in a pan of *essence* and set it on fire just to see what would happen. Luckily he had enough sense to move away, for the cylinder, which was of course a rifle grenade, exploded and tore a hole in the ground as large as a bushel basket. The French mechanics and Decupert, the lieutenant's secretary, none of whom have been up near the trenches, felt sure the Boches were shelling the village again and wouldn't leave their *abri* for fully an hour.

It rather pleases us to learn that the Frenchmen are just as scared as we are when they go out under fire for the first time. When we were putting a whole new front system on Haven's car near the entrance to the *château* the night of the second attack, August and Leon were there to help. Every time when Leon would start to use his hammer, August would seize his arm and say "*Doucement*, the Boches are just behind that house and they will get us with hand grenades if we make any noise." Then, before we were through a heavy bombardment started up behind the church, perhaps one hundred and fifty yards away. And each time that we heard the whistling of a shell someone would yell "Duck fellows, it's a big boy this time." August and Leon seemed to understand perfectly; at mention of the word "duck" they would always disappear beneath the ambulance, and remain there until all was quiet again.

To tell the truth however, it isn't much fun waiting around with nothing to do while a car is being repaired. It's bad enough when you are busy working on the car. But when you have to wait for someone else to finish a job, you get a little nervous, especially when they are peppering the road. The star shells also worry one. You feel that the Boches have spotted you each time and you try to figure the number of seconds before a shell will arrive. . . . If we find it is impossible to repair a car sufficiently to tow it back to Dombasle, or even to Montzèville, it has to be left out there on the road to the mercy of the enemy. If they don't shell it, we fix it up the next evening; but if they do, it's goodbye, ambulance.

April 13th. Dombasle.

We are to leave soon for *repos* going to some village southwest of here. We may go tomorrow, or perhaps the next day; but at all events, our sojourn here will soon be over, and we will never return. The division has suffered tremendously and they certainly deserve a rest.

Five of our men got the "*Croix de guerre*" for work during the first two attacks. We had hoped that the section as a whole would be cited, instead of certain individuals being picked out from the rest. But it didn't happen that way. Houston, Craig, McLane, Walker and Gillespie were the lucky fellows. Their citations came yesterday afternoon from the general of the division and we celebrated in the evening with a big dinner.

The sausage at Jouy was brought down this morning by a Boche aviator. I was standing outside the cantonment with "Ott" Kann when the anti-aircraft gun started. Soon we caught sight of a tiny German plane, ten or twelve thousand feet above us. He was heading straight for the balloon, and descending so rapidly that for a while we thought he was falling. By this time the pilot of the sausage had signalled his men on the ground of his danger and the great drum was reeling in wire cable at the rate of twenty miles an hour. But this was not fast enough to escape from the hands of the clever aviator. For suddenly, while he was still a thousand yards above the balloon, he opened up his machine gun. We could hear its rat-tat-tats very clearly, although he was five miles away. Two or three of the flaming bullets happened to pierce the hydrogen bag, and in an instant it was turned into a mass of flames. Before the pilot was able to jump from his basket and save himself in his parachute, he was overcome by the gas and flames. Barney Faith went over afterwards and found his aneroid barometer.

Benney and I were talking before the fire in his room today (they don't cut up their wood as we do; instead, they lug a twenty foot beam into the room, place one end on the hearth and as it burns, shove it further in, Indian Fashion), and Gilmore was attempting to make hot chocolate from a cake which he couldn't shave down with a piece of *éclat*, when a knock came at the door. He yelled "*Entrez*," and, as the door slowly opened, we saw an old French couple standing on the threshold. This had been their home six months before, and now they had returned to look upon the wreckage. The woman wept when she saw the shell hole through the ceiling, the broken furniture which we were burning on our fire and the heap of old family treasures lying in one corner. We said nothing, we couldn't say anything; but as they sadly departed, the man muttered, "It is not very nice but after the war we will——" and we heard no more.

Benney and I were silent and Gilmore forgot about his cocoa for a few minutes. It had never occurred to us before when we tore a house to pieces for firewood, and carted off all the books and ornaments for souvenirs, that people like these had actually lived in them or would ever return. War becomes a little sadder, a little more real now, after we have seen what the civilian population has suffered. Before, Dombasle was only a mass of ruined buildings. Now we see in it the destruction of hundreds of happy homes, and the scattering abroad of all the inhabitants.

This week's American mail arrived today. I received four letters from the family, and one from Helen. She tells me the long promised socks have finally been finished. But instead of sending them in the usual manner, she is going to mail them in two separate packages, a week or ten days apart, so that (this is the brilliant idea) if one sock is lost at sea, she will have only one more to knit.

One of the new ten inch railway guns passed through town today and fired about fifty practice shots up to the Boche trenches on Hill 304, about seven miles distant. Bradley and I heard before that the affair was going to come off and got down to the tracks just as they began to fire. There were two cars in the outfit, one for the shells, and the other for the gun itself. Great jacks were propped under the south side of the car, presumably to keep it from being knocked over by the recoil. The shells, which happened to be "220's," were shoved from the other car up to the breech in a long trough. The brass powder casings were being carried by hand and pushed into the gun immediately after the projectile itself had been put in place.

The men were working well and sending four or five shots a minute, which isn't bad for a gun of that calibre. One of the officers standing near told us if we got directly behind the gun and twenty or thirty feet away from it we would see the shell emerging from the mouth. We couldn't find it at all at first but after a few trials, we managed to locate it almost before we heard the explosion. It looked like a small black ball and appeared to be shooting directly upwards; and if you strained your eyes you could see it for eight and sometimes even ten seconds.

*April 14th.* Dombasle.

The final orders have come. We will leave Dombasle tomorrow morning and go to some town near Epernay where the division will be *en repos*. Those of us who were not on duty today had to wash our cars again and then load each machine with Ford parts, *essence* (gasoline) cans, and things like stoves and supplies which we carry from place to place.

Old 464 has sunk way down on her springs with three twenty gallon cans of gasoline and a box of the Frenchmen's tools.

I was on duty for the last time at Esnes yesterday. It was pretty quiet in the morning, when I was poking about in the shell holes behind the *château*, hunting for time fuses. Lloyd and Harrison came out on Kann's car about eleven, on a camera hike. We had lunch with LeFevre in his *abri*. Afterwards I asked M. Bouvier if he would take us up into the second line trenches, or at least to the top of Hill 304, but he was a trifle reluctant about it and finally went off somewhere by himself. Another chap, a *brancardier* named Foker whom I knew fairly well, had heard us talking and as soon as Bouvier left, offered to go up with us. We jumped at the chance and set out immediately. Fully exposed to the enemy, who were less than one mile away, we started up the hill, which commences a few rods behind the post.

As we drew near the top we obtained a magnificent view of the whole surrounding country. Before us lay the summit of Hill 304, whose clayish brown soil had been ploughed up again and again during the three years the mighty struggles have been waged over it. To the east rose *Mort Homme*. Along its gentle sloping crest we could distinguish the first line German trenches, and thirty or forty yards below them, the French.

Now and then a German shell exploded in the valley below, just to let us know the war was still going on. We had only gone a short distance beyond this point when it became necessary to enter a *boyau* or communication trench. No Man's Land lay four hundred yards in front of us over the next slope and although we couldn't be seen here from a German outpost, we had to be very careful; for nothing lay between us and the Boche machine guns in the valley towards *Mort Homme*.

Foker thought it better not to go in the open any longer since there were four of us together and it was a pretty clear day. Walking through the windings of the trench, we descended into the ravine which the French called the "Valley of Death." It got very muddy near the bottom, especially where sections of the trench had been caved in by shells. Finally, after we had sunk in up to our knees several times, Foker decided that we could take a chance on walking in the open again. A couple of shrapnel burst above us but it was such a short distance now to the second lines that we didn't bother about going back to the *boyau* again.

We came to the "*Poste de Secours*" which we recognized some distance away by the Red Cross flag, stuck in a lump of clay outside the *abri*. We stopped for a few minutes to get warm and also to inquire if it would be possible to go to the first line trenches. One *poilu* volunteered to take us up, but the doctor in charge told us it would be safer to make the trip at night. The trenches were in such bad shape from the last two attacks that one of us would very likely be potted by a German sniper in passing through a destroyed section. We were thankful for their kindness and I promised to return at nine that evening, if there were no "*grand couchés*" to take down to Ville.

When we left the post a severe snowstorm was blowing which permitted us to make the entire trip back to the *château* in the open. No souvenir hunter could imagine anything more wonderful. The whole side of the hill was literally strewn with hand-grenades, unexploded German shells of every size, huge trench torpedoes, ready to be sent on their last journey, and bushels of *éclat*, compression bands and time fuses. I found a perfect top of a German "150" (six inch) shell, loaded with shrapnel: but it was so heavy I had to drop it after a few hundred yards. I also picked up five Boche *fusées*, some pieces of compression band from a ten inch shell and the base of a torpedo. I put them in the side box of my car as soon as I got to the post again. Bouvier heard about our plans for returning in the evening a short time after we arrived and was so opposed to our going that we gave up the idea for the moment. Sammy Lloyd and Harrison started for Montzèville not long afterwards and I went back to Dombasle, where I now am, Bradley having relieved me at half-past eight. It will be hard, leaving our cantonment here tomorrow. For although we will be delighted to have a short rest in some quiet little village, nevertheless our work here has been very interesting and we do not look forward with much pleasure to the *repos* life of Longeville and Jubécourt.

CHAPTER 3

# In the Argonne Forest

*April 15th*, 1917.                        Senard *En Repos*

A great many things have happened since we left Dombasle, yesterday morning. Last night we stayed in a little place named Waly and then this morning we went on through Triacourt to Senard where the doctor told us we were to stay during *repos*. We naturally expected that we would remain here two or three weeks. So we unpacked all the cars and spent most of the morning making our sleeping quarters in the barn comfortable. Suddenly, when four of us were playing horseshoes near our *salle à manger* the news came that we were to move in one hour, to join another division in a new sector.

This was a shock to all of us for it meant not only leaving our friends the *brancardiers* of the G.B.D. (stretcher-bearer corps) but also M. Holland, our doctor, who had been so good to us, and all the *poilus* in the division with whom we had become acquainted during the two months we had been with them. Two of the Frenchmen are leaving the section today; Lieutenant Bayart, to go to America on some business with which he was connected before the war, and kind little Monsieur Phillipe who is to be transferred to another service.

I am now writing this in the front seat of my car. We have said farewell to our friends and have formed the cars in convoy along the village street. The order to start will soon be given, and we will leave the old Hundred and Thirty-second forever. Iselin has whistled. I can write no more, for the fellows are cranking their cars, and Number One is already on its way.

*April 28th.*                                Ste. Menehould.

It is almost two weeks since we left our division at Senard. We are now attached to another, the Seventy-first, with our cantonment in

1. In a mine under "No Man's Land," fifteen feet from the Boche trenches. Several tons of powder are piled up in the background. Two of the *poilus*, listening with microphones to the conversation of the German's across the way, will set off the mine at the proper moment.
2. In another mine with Amulot the "Happy" *poilu* in the centre. The men are working with the aid of a carbide lamp.

1. A MINE CRATER AFTER THE EXPLOSION. IT IS MORE THAN TWO HUNDRED FEET LONG. FORTY FRENCH SOLDIERS WERE KILLED HERE.
2. A SUPPLY STATION IN A FRONT LINE TRENCH AT LA HARAZEE. HERE ARE COLLECTED PERISCOPES, HAND AND RIFLE GRENADES, CORKSCREW BARBED-WIRE STAKES, AND RIFLES. A GAS ALARM GONG HANGS ABOVE THE *POILU* ON THE LEFT.
3. MIDSUMMER IN THE ARGONNE FOREST.

Ste. Menehould. We evacuate two front line posts, La Harazee and St. Thomas, about fourteen miles north of here, and one relay which they call Suniat. There are always two cars at each post instead of one as we used to have at Esnes and Post Two. The hills afford wonderful protection for the roads. At La Harazee our cars are only four hundred yards from the Boche lines and at St. Thomas less than half a mile. As far as I can learn, there hasn't been much heavy fighting here for over a year and I am afraid we are in for six, or perhaps eight weeks of easy work.

Craig and I were sent to La Harazee the second day after we arrived here. We started exploring the place as soon as we got out of our cars. The quarters which they had given us we found to be a very comfortable *abri*, dug into the side of a steep hill, in Pueblo Indian fashion. Directly opposite our doorway stood the morgue and the Regiment refuse heap. We soon discovered the *brancardiers'* kitchen where we were to eat, and immediately made friends with the cook. Waiting around the post became very dull, and when the sergeant said that he didn't believe we would have a run before noon, we got his permission to take a short walk in the trenches which begin about one hundred feet behind our quarters.

In barely five minutes we came to the second lines. While we were standing here, wondering whether we ought to go any further alone, a *poilu* from a nearby machine post came up. By tactful words and many cigarettes we got him to go with us up to the first line. He took us two or three kilometres along the front, explaining everything as we went from one place to another. I had my first peek through a field periscope at some German trenches fifty yards away, and at a listening post, which the Boches only use at night, twenty yards distant. We learned exactly how the communication trenches intertwine with the first, second and third lines, how there are grenade and observation posts a few yards apart, and where the deep *abris* are located in which thousands of cylinders of gas lie stored, ready at a moment's notice to be sent over to the German lines.

Our guide told us the French had sent over a big attack last week and that the Boches would probably reply as soon as they got a favourable wind. While we were talking at this place a little toy balloon came sailing overhead, from the enemy's lines, apparently to test the speed and velocity of the wind. When we returned to the post, we learned that it had brought over a number of German newspapers commenting upon the war and making various suggestions for peace.

There were also several French papers, printed in the Ardennes, which is captured territory. I managed to get one of the latter, and found to my surprise, that three whole pages were devoted to the names of French soldiers in the hands of the Germans. The name of each man, his military and his regiment number, were all given. But of course the whole journal had been very heavily censored by the enemy authorities.

It was a poor attempt, however, to conceal their plans for a gas attack. After this he showed us places where there was a network of barbed-wire, above the trench to block the way in case of a German attack; and machine gun positions at the end of certain *boyaux* which sweep the whole trench if necessary. We then learned how to throw hand grenades, how to send up star shells and to fire rifle grenades, and how necessary it was to talk quietly on account of the proximity of the enemy. Luckily I had my camera with me and I took picture after picture of the things we saw. When we were obliged to return to La Harazee, the guide gave us an automatic revolver, which he had taken from a German officer. We paid him twenty *francs* for it. It would very likely have sold for a hundred *marks* in Berlin.

Two days later I went to La Harazee again. I had gone about half way when a *poilu* stopped me and asked for a ride. We are not supposed to carry any persons except wounded, but sometimes we take pity on a poor fellow and give him a lift. This particular man was returning to the front from his leave of absence: he had been walking all day and I thought it wouldn't hurt to carry him a few miles. He was a very interesting fellow and turned out to be connected with a still more interesting service. He was one of the operators of a new device for receiving the enemy's telephone messages by means of sound waves through the earth. They have a sort of wireless outfit stationed half a mile behind the first lines, and to this are connected several long copper wires which extend to the German "*fil de fer*" (barbed-wire) out in No Man's Land, which is about as close as they can get to the German telephone system without being detected. With this apparatus they are able to hear the Boche messages very distinctly. But he told me that both sides now send all of their important news by courier, for the Germans have recently discovered a similar device and they blockade each other's moves very successfully. However, it was used for several months by the French and English before their friends across No Man's Land knew anything about it.

I carried the biggest load I have ever had in the car when I came back to Ste. Menehould the next day. Besides five *blessés* including a captain, a couple of artillery men and a poor fellow with the measles, were Williams who had come along to show me a new post in the woods, the rifles, helmets and packs of every soldier and the officer's trunk, an empty *pinard* barrel and four *ravitaillement* boxes. It was not a simple task to load this into a little Ford ambulance and climb those long hard hills on the return journey. However the car stood up to her task like a real automobile and I am proud of her. As soon as I got to Ste. Menehould I took the captain to "1—71," as the big hospital in the main square of the city is called. Then I left three of those remaining at the H. O. E. near the railroad station; and had to lug Monsieur Measles five miles further on, to the contagious hospital at Verrieres.

*May 2nd.*  Quarters at Ste. Menehould.

Gilmore and I have been printing pictures since dark; we have rigged up a temporary dark-room in our barn and do all our photographic work here. We use a candle behind some coloured paper for a red light, and an old carbide auto lamp instead of a Mazda bulb for printing. Naturally, we have no running water but carry all that we use for two blocks in our radiator buckets. Of course we might send our films into Paris to be developed but then there is the chance of losing them in the mails or at the overworked "Kodaks" office. And especially since some of the photos are mighty valuable to us, we prefer to do them ourselves.

After supper we had a regular rough and tumble circus out behind the *salle à manger*. Frazer and Ray Eaton were feeling happy after a bottle of *pinard* apiece and we were all in for a good time. Somehow or other Eaton got the idea that he was a young Hercules and for a good quarter of an hour stood with his head through the centre rung of a ladder and tried to swing the thing around with a fellow on each end. Of course it was a strain on him and after three or four rounds he would fall to the ground exhausted. Then Frazer bet me a bottle of champagne that he could pull his foot up over his head before I could. I was somewhat soberer than he was, and managed to beat him to it. But he kept stubbornly at it and finally got his foot over and several inches further down his back than I had. The judges called the affair a draw. After this we tried climbing a ladder without support, crawling all the way around a table without touching the ground and jumping over a broomstick held by both hands. A large and interested crowd of townspeople and soldiers collected to watch these queer, rough games in which we Americans seemed to delight.

I spent thirteen cents this afternoon to have my hair clipped and get a shave. The latter was the first one in three months and took off a fairly respectable moustache. Then, to make the overhauling complete, I took an eighteen cent bath at the Hospital "Mixte," where all the Algerians and Moroccans go. This is really the first time I have seen a tub since I left the Espagne at Bordeaux almost four months ago.

"Montzie" committed suicide this morning. He carelessly stepped into an open sewer near the cantonment shortly after he had left the dining-room and that was the last time he was seen alive. It was rather an untimely ending after his hairbreadth escapes on the Esnes road, and after his sleeping on stretchers oozing blood in the old *abri* at Post Two. Montzèville, I wouldn't have thought it of you, you ugly little mongrel pup.

The fine "*Ecole des Garcons*" here in Ste. Menehould has been requisitioned by the government for hospital purposes and school is being held just at present in a wooden shack behind our cantonment. Every morning at recess forty or fifty of the little fellows flock around our cars, playing marbles and spinning tops. One would think that they were girls, in their funny little black aprons. They seem rather fond of me for I have taken a number of pictures of them at play; then the other morning I threw down to them, from the loft in the barn, about fifty tiny American flags which father sent to me. There was one grand scramble for them and of course some went away with more than their share. Now I can hardly walk to the *epicerie* without some little fellow asking me for a *petit drapeau*. And if I ask him what he did with the one he got in the scramble the day before, he says he tried to keep it, but his little sister cried for it so when he got home that he had to give it to her. . . . They are always eager to talk. Several days ago one little chap came up to my car in which I was sitting, reading a letter from home, and asked me how old I was. He was rather surprised when I told him seventeen and couldn't understand why I had come over at that age. He had a brother eighteen, who wasn't to join the army for three months yet.

We aren't nearly so busy as we would like to be. Three days of the week we loaf around Ste. Menehould and then we are on duty for the next twenty-four hours at one of the posts. At times we work on our cars or hammer out souvenirs from Boche bullets and pieces of shell. A few of us are fond of quoits and play every day on a little island in the Aisne, across from our quarters. In the afternoon we drop around

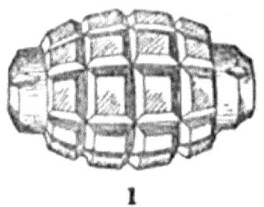

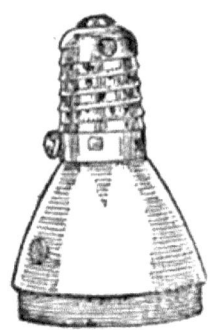

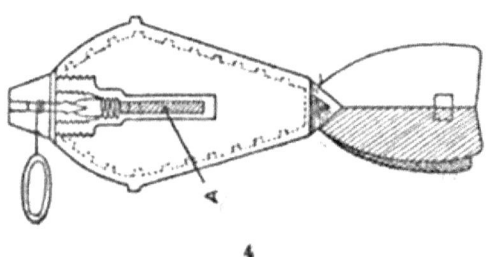

*See opposite page.*

1. French "citron" hand grenade. The cap, which has been removed, is screwed on to one end; before throwing the grenade, the cap is struck with the hand or knocked against some hard object. It explodes six or seven seconds later, and breaks up into as many pieces as there are squares. It is quite similar to the English "Mill's" grenade.

2. French rifle grenade, which has become very popular at the front. It is placed in a little funnel-shaped steel cylinder which fits over the barrel of a rifle; the bullet passes through the centre, explodes the cap projecting from the knob on the right, and flies off into the air. The grenade itself is propelled by the escaping gases, and, travelling anywhere from 50 to 200 or 300 yards, is exploded a few seconds afterwards, by the time fuse ignited by the cap.

3. The time fuse and head of a French "75" (3 inch) shell. The fuse is ignited by a cap and trigger within the fuse at the moment the shell leaves the gun. This ignites the powder, wrapped in a spiral coil running from the top of the fuse to the screw on the left. This burns until it comes to the hole punched at the second (time unit mark on the brass covering) at which the shell is to explode. Then the flame passes into the shell itself and explodes the "B. S. P." or high explosive powder by igniting the last big cap.

4. A two pound French trench torpedo which is shot out of a small gun by means of compressed air and hurled a distance of 200 or 300 yards. It is exploded by the fulminate of mercury cap, A, which in turn is set off by the trigger. The ring regulates the position of the latter and the spring keeps the cap and trigger separated.

to the *patisserie* near the Hotel de Ville, if we have any money, and get Marie, the attractive little waitress there, to bring us a tray of cream tarts and lemonade—occasionally we experiment on something stronger. But on Tuesdays and Wednesdays it is closed, as are all the *patisseries* and candy shops in France: we cannot even buy milk chocolate at an *epicerie*, so we have to be content with our regular fare.

The other evening, Bradley who comes from Berkley, California, and Tenney, the only fellow in the section who has a smaller moustache than my own, set out with me for a stroll in the moonlight when it was really time to be in bed. We talked of the war, of section life and many other things; and when an hour had passed we were still going on. We reached the summit of a high hill overlooking Ste. Menehould some three miles away, and sat down on a grassy bank, to rest and to watch the star shells breaking in the Champagne Sector. Just as we arose to begin our return journey the searchlight on the hill in the city threw its great shaft of light into the sky and played it back and forth across the heavens.

Then a shot from the anti-aircraft gun beside it broke the quiet of the night. We could not locate the enemy aeroplane for it never rested in one place. We were on top of a little knoll and could see very clearly the flash from the gun in Ste. Menehould, followed by the report twelve seconds later and then immediately after this, the bright glare from the exploding shrapnel a mile above us. They fired only a few shots, however, for they were unable to locate the plane on account of its great height. As we walked home the nightingales were singing. They make one forget about the war and think of France three years ago, when men instead of women were ploughing in the fields, when Dombasle and Esnes and St. Thomas were happy villages, not dull piles of stone. The *poilu* too, dreams of those days and hopes and prays for the time when he can return to his family and again resume his normal life.

*May 7th.* St. Thomas.

This is my first time on duty here. I have been twice to La Harazee and once to Suniat. They call the place St. Thomas because of a little village of that name which used to be here. I guess it has been totally destroyed by German fire, for I have never seen anything of the houses. There is, however, part of a wall standing near the post, which looks as though it might have belonged to a church. The post itself is one of the best we have ever had. It is an old gravel-pit in the side of a hill, and is very well protected on three sides. Next to us is the *abri* of a colonel of the two hundred and twenty-first regiment. It is a fine one, reinforced with cement and has an attractive flower garden in front of it. The latter contains a lot of unexploded Boche shells, which have fallen nearby and which some generous soul has brought to the colonel to use as boundary marks for his garden. Then not far from the spot where I left my car is a deep well of fine cool water. I mean to take a couple of gallons back to Ste. Menehould with me, for the water there comes from the Aisne and is very poor.

After I got acquainted with the *brancardiers* who seemed to be "*midis*" from the South of France, I set out on a walk in the trenches, and was gone about three hours. At one place in a first line trench I got a wonderful view of No Man's Land and the Boche trenches. In the background stood the ruins of Servon, through which their third line runs.

A heavy bombardment began as I was leaving and shell after shell whistled overhead, apparently going toward St. Thomas. Sad to say, it was all over before I arrived and a lot of new holes around the post and everybody sticking pretty close to his *abri* were the only signs that anything unusual had happened. While we were eating lunch a *blessé* came in who had lost the thumb and first finger of each hand half an hour before while attempting to unload a Boche grenade. He suffered terribly but never made a whimper during the long ride into Suniat. After I saw this fellow I thought of what one little grenade had done to him and wondered why it was we take chance after chance in unloading stuff, just for souvenirs. A couple of fingers missing or a scarred face makes a more lasting souvenir than an old shell, but one you wouldn't be so proud of.

We had a lively time at supper tonight, in our *abri* next to the post. Instead of cooking their own food the lazy *brancardiers* get it all prepared from one of the big kitchen sections just a few hundred yards from here. One of the dishes was fried potatoes. There weren't enough forks to go round, so we ate them with our fingers. One old fellow from Toulouse who told me afterwards that he was forty-eight years old, bragged that he hadn't tasted a drop of water for ten years. They joked all during the meal about their wine and told me I'd never be a real *poilu* (the word really means "hairy one") if I didn't drink *pinard*. So finally I let them pour me out a glass and we gave a toast to the speedy ending of the war.

1. The shelter of the little gun which shoots small trench torpedoes by means of compressed air.
2. A gas attack this evening? This poilu is learning, by means of his weathervane and an instrument for recording the velocity of the wind, whether or not he can launch an attack.
3. Gilmore in the steel turret of an observation post, twenty yards in front of the first lines.

1. An American made ten ton truck, so camouflaged with cubist painting in green, brown and yellow that it is rendered invisible at half a mile.
2. A gunboat on the Châlons-Prunay canal. It carries two five-inch cannon and a number of machine guns.
3. A machine depot in Champagne, where 60,000 shells are stored; each pile is carefully camouflaged with pine boughs.

*May 15th,* 1917.                              Hotel Continental, Paris.

This heading certainly must look funny in my diary. The last entry was written while eating lunch with a crowd of *brancardiers* about a half a mile from the German lines and this one, in an actually civilized room at the Hotel Continental. It happened that my *permission* fell due the day after I came back from St. Thomas and I left the Section at Ste. Menehould to spend eight happy days in Paris. It was a long hot ride into Paris and we had to stand up all the way. But it was wonderful to get there and even more wonderful to take a hot bath at the hotel and then sleep between a real pair of linen sheets for fourteen hours.

Paris is happier than when we left. There are no coal worries now and the markets are overflowing with fresh spring vegetables and fruits. Our entry into the war seems to have cheered the people immensely. Everywhere you go there are American flags hanging from the windows. They think about it so much and talk about it so much that one would suppose we had a million men over here already.

I have had a wonderful time ever since I arrived.

For when I am not playing tennis with some most attractive English girls at their country club on an island in the Seine, I am chasing out to Versailles for an afternoon or promenading with some friend in the *Bois de Boulogne*. Every evening Anderson and I get together and, starting out with a marvellous meal at Foyots or Drouants, we end up with the opera and a *café* afterwards. The authorities are very strict about meats, sugar and certain vegetables in the restaurants; but you can't go hungry if you are willing to pay the price.

The field service is growing very rapidly and has taken over an annex in Rue Le Kain. Instead of receiving fifteen or twenty new men each week as they were doing when we came last February they are getting one hundred now. Since it is impossible to send them all out in Ambulance Sections, Andrew and Galatti have organized a group of truck sections which will handle ammunition and supplies behind the lines. It won't be quite as exciting as our work but it will be very interesting and certainly very helpful to the French army.

Andy and I went to the Gaumont Palace in Clichy tonight. They had advertised a big movie called *L'Invasion des Etats Unis*! We thought we were going to see a remarkable picture, but it turned out to be the old *Battle Cry of Peace*, which I had seen in New York two years before. The French audience, however, thought it quite wonderful and applauded continually throughout the show. They understand, far better than we do in America, its real meaning. Andy had to leave early and since the Metro had stopped I walked back to Rue Raynouard afterwards. It was long after midnight when I got there. The door was locked at Twenty-one, so I had to climb over the wall. Two other *permissionaires* who had been down in the Latin Quarter came up while I was struggling to get in and the three of us managed to get over together.

I will probably go back to the section tomorrow with Williams and Allen. We are to get our "*Ordre de Movement*" from the office of the Army Automobile Service, next to the Gobelin tapestry works, in the morning and leave from the *Gare de l'Est* at noon.

May 22.                                                                       Ste. Menehould again.

There was a big package from home awaiting me at the bureau on my return from Paris. I found a wonderful lot of eatables inside when I opened it. A few of the contents I could have bought in France but the maple sugar, grape-nuts and peanut butter were purely American. The sugar was delicious and enjoyed by everyone in the section. Even the rats got their share. Last evening I put a lump at the head of my bed and Gilmore says he was awakened several times during the night by their clamour as they played on top of me. But I wasn't disturbed by them at all. I was sound asleep, dreaming of the good times I'd had in Paris. I had a lot of fun, too, with the Frenchmen over the peanut butter. I told them that it was American mustard, very expensive and much superior to their own, and let one of them try a little on a piece of bread. He threw it away in disgust after one bite and said we could eat it if we liked, but that it tasted rotten and he would stick to the French variety. They couldn't make out the grape-nuts either and seemed to think it was made from the crumbs of some hard material like their army bread.

Benney had a remarkable escape one day last week, while I was away. He was driving one of Mrs. Harry Payne Whitney's cars, Number 78, through Vienne la Ville, on his way home from St. Thomas when a Boche shell exploded ten feet from him. Luckily it was at the rear of his car or he would have been killed instantly. As it was, his klaxon was torn off and the whole back of the ambulance was filled with *éclat*.

Eaton has finally come back from the hospital at Ville sur Couzances. That little scalding at Dombasle last March laid him up for two long months. He tells lots of funny stories about his treatment there and claims to be the champion endurance wearer of winter flannels of the American Ambulance. He wore the same pair of woollen underwear for three months.

Payne came in from La Harazee this noon, grouchy as old Scrooge himself. And it was not until the happy-go-lucky Frazer ambled into our apartments an hour later with a broad grin on his face that we learned what was troubling Payne. It seems that the two had been at La Harazee together and Frazer started out for town with two *malades* and one *couché* when the relief man came at ten-thirty. He had a close shave at Vienne la Ville where, as usual, the Boches were shelling the main street of the village. He would have gone through at top speed if he had not noticed a poor beggar, with a bad cut in the arm, lying in the gutter. Of course he stopped to pick him up. While he was trying to lug the fellow over to his ambulance several more shells landed in the road in front of him and Frazer hardly knew whether he ought to run off and leave the man there or not.

Just then a cloud of dust appeared in the distance which turned out to be Payne, trying to imitate Dario Resta. Frazer yelled at him when he got closer, to stop and help him with the *blessé*.... But Payne didn't notice him at all. He was too busy trying to keep the car on the road. Frazer had to get along as well as he could by himself and it took him five or six minutes to get his case arranged on a stretcher and loaded into the car. The Boches were still shelling the place when he left but he managed to get his load out safely. He found Payne waiting for him on the top of the next hill. And when Frazer asked him why the devil he hadn't stopped to help him down in the village, the other replied that he thought it would make such a wonderful picture with Frazer loading in wounded, with shells breaking on all sides, that he had just gone on about half a mile further, and then turned around and photographed it. I presume Payne is peeved because he did such a crazy childish trick. He certainly ought to be.

Almost every day a Boche aviator flies overhead. This morning one dropped seven bombs in the town but fortunately no one was killed. Two fell very near the cantonment, and as we were awakened by the explosions, we heard little pieces of *éclat* come pattering down on the roof. A soldier in one of the neighbouring houses had his pillow torn away and the wall above him pierced in fifty places by steel splinters. He received only a couple of scratches, however. Everyone, especially the little fellows in the school, delight in watching such a fight. They clap and shout "*tres bien*" if a shell bursts near the enemy's plane and if it finally escapes they console themselves with "just wait, we will get him the next time."

Lundquist and I visited the aviation field today, hoping to get a short trip in an observation plane. The officers were very polite and told us everything about the machines but couldn't allow us to go up on account of orders, which they apologized for not being able to break.

I spent several hours this afternoon grinding down 464's valves and scraping out the carbon from the cylinders. It was a dirty job and a rather long one but well worth the effort. Now she runs fifty *per cent* better, and when I gave her a trial run afterwards, she took the worst hills around here on high.

Sammy Lloyd told me tonight about the three American girls who were here while I was away on leave. They had been connected with a clearing house in Paris, and wanting to see a little of the front before they returned to the States, they got papers from some high official allowing them to take a three days' tour along the front, and started out for the war zone. They came to Ste. Menehould on the second day, and one of the fellows offered to drive them out to one of our posts. They went to St. Thomas, had a peek at the trenches and No Man's Land and rushed back to the city again. Possibly, they intend to lecture at home on conditions in France and life in the trenches!

*May 28th.*                                                   Suniat Relay-Post.

Suniat is a queer place, sort of a hospital and yet for most cases, merely a relay post. Tom Orr and I have been on duty here since yesterday at noon. We had one run apiece during the night with some *blessés* from a little *coup de main*. This is a very small attack where a patrol of fifteen or twenty men are sent over to the enemy's lines to bring back prisoners. Later these men are questioned and much information, such as the movement of troops and the location of machine-guns is obtained.

It is a beautiful Spring day here. The trees are covered with leaves once more and the fields seem brighter than they were two weeks ago. I was talking to the *mèdecin major* this morning, bragging about the huge apple-trees we grow in America. I carelessly used the expression *pomme de terre* for the word apple, and he laughingly told me that there weren't any potato trees in France. Several of the officers here have asked me if I knew of any attractive American girls who would be willing to correspond with them. This seems to be an old custom among the French soldiers, and a very good one.

For a cheerful letter from their *marraine*, as they call her, is a great treat to these men.

Two days ago, when I was at La Harazee, I visited the trenches at night and spent several hours in the first lines. I had promised Amulot, who belongs to the "Sappers" and lives in an *abri* near ours, that I would go to his mine the next time I was on duty here and take some flashlights of him working underground. He called for me at eight o'clock and from then on I had a most interesting evening. We took the same communication trench to the first lines which I had used before and then walked some distance along this before we came to the entrance of the mine. Here he said a few words to the guard. After this we went down a long series of steps, until we were fully thirty feet underground. It was very cold and damp and water trickled down in little streams from the ceiling. Then he took me through a long passage in the direction of the Boche trenches, and finally stopped in a little room which seemed to be the end of the tunnel.

By the light of the *pigeon* lamp which he held in his hand I could see two *poilus*, one piling up powder in a great stack in a corner and the other who had a pair of microphone receivers on his head, listening to something very intently. Amulot whispered to me that the Boche trenches were only twenty feet above us here and that one of their counter mines was just ten feet away. The man with the phones, he told me, was trying to learn what the Germans were doing across the way; he could hear them digging and even talking, with his apparatus. If they continued to work there much longer the French would soon set off their mine and blow up every Hun within a hundred yards.

I got a photo of them at work, with a sack of earth for a support for my camera, and my gasmask held in one hand above my head as a tray for the flashlight powder. It was pitch-black when we emerged into the open again. In front of us a couple of Frenchmen were repairing barbed-wire out in No Man's Land and to the left a hand-grenade duel was in progress. I thought it was time to get back to the post but Amulot said no. He was picture-crazy and had to take me to two other mines, and also to a place where they had a new trench gun which shoots funny little torpedoes by compressed air. This took up fully an hour more and when I again remarked that I had better be leaving, he said that he wanted me to hear a Boche machine gun first. And what did he do but dash out into No Man's Land and pound on some stones with a pick so that the enemy would hear him. Luckily no star shell went up very close to him while he was out, or he would surely have been potted. I heard the machine gun very distinctly, however.

I think he had had more *pinard* for supper than was good for him. It was long after midnight when I got back to La Harazee. To my surprise I found Haven had been sent to Suniat with three *couchés*, and not ten minutes later they brought down a load for me. I thanked my stars that it had not come while I was out with Amulot. On the way down I learned that the *blessés* I was carrying had been wounded in an outpost near the mine in which I took the last picture and at the very time we were down in it.

There is great rivalry in the section to see who can do the most exciting thing in the trenches at La Harazee. Several days ago I hung around an observation post about fifty yards from the enemy's lines until I finally got a glimpse of the steel plate of a Boche post and apparently the eye of a sniper behind it. It disappeared after a while and a minute later I saw the smoke from his cigarette floating upwards some distance further down the trench. . . . Then on Saturday, when Ott Kann and Harrison were there, they yelled over to a Boche and had a short conversation with him and ended with the heads of both sides above the trench. . . . Gilmore and Payne thought they would go them one better, and the next time actually go over with a lot of bread and chocolate; of course they intended to make arrangements beforehand to meet him half-way; and since they both speak German this would not be hard. The idea may seem absurd but it has been done a good many times by the French and they thought they could work it too. However, I am afraid they can't for if they told the officers they would be stopped, and if they should go without their knowing it, they might be brought up as spies when it was found out.

Hang it all! It's ten o'clock, and all the lights have gone out.

CHAPTER 4

# "En Repos," and in Champagne

*June 5th*, 1917.                                           Les Grandes Loges.
On the first day of June we departed from Ste. Menehould for good and all. Section Thirteen which last month was worked to death in Champagne, has taken our place. We are delighted to be able to try our luck at some real action once more. The little town where we are now staying, Les Grandes Loges, lies on the main road between Châlons and Reims. We shall probably remain here for a week *en repos* and then go up to the front for three or four weeks of heavy action. As usual in the smaller towns our quarters are in a barn and our cars are parked in the courtyard; there is a high hill behind the village, and every day we go to the summit to watch the artillery duels around Mont Cornillet and Moronvilliers, eight miles away. Last evening we saw a German gas attack roll over the French lines; great clouds of a creamy, yellowish vapour, stretching along the lines for a mile or more, were carried forward by the wind and poured into every nook and cranny of our trenches.

In the midst of this a great puff of black smoke arose from the hill and a minute later we heard the report. It came either from a mine, or a "420," which the Boches occasionally send over. After we had crawled into bed in the barn, a German aviator shot down out of the sky and played his machine gun up and down the village street. He couldn't have been more than four hundred feet high for we heard the "rack-a-tack" of his machine gun as plainly as if it had been in the court behind the barn. This was a new trick to us, but the old lady who lives next door says they have been doing it all Spring. She tells me she is eighty years old, but every day I see her working in her garden. She is very cheerful and seems to like the work, but she is shy, and hates to have people watch her. The other morning I wanted to take her picture and it took ten minutes of careful persuasion to get her consent.

Today we walked to the canal four miles south of the village and went in swimming. There were a couple of gun boats waiting here, to be sent up towards Prunay; and it gave one a queer feeling, emerging from a dive, to have this awkward steel monitor looking him in the face.

*June 10th.*                      Recy (near Châlons-sur-Marne)

Recy is the deadest little town in the Department of the Marne. They are therefore punishing the Two-Twenty-First, and consequently us at the same time, by billeting us here for the *repos*. I am afraid that we are going to have a mighty dull month, loafing around the cantonment and taking a *malade* run once a week.

Sometimes there is a little more than this, however. We were all moping around the cantonment yesterday, when Decupert, the lieutenant's clerk, came in and said orders had just come from Bouy, a place ten miles north of here, to send out fifteen ambulances at once: the Boches were shelling the town, and we had to evacuate the hospital. There was a mad stampede to the cars, and in five minutes fifteen little Fords were racing wildly over the hills towards Bouy. The bombardment was over when we arrived. The Boches appeared to have been testing a new long-range gun, and dropped about forty of the big shells into the town from a battery fourteen miles away; but no great damage was done.

One shell which dropped in the courtyard of the hospital, made a crater twenty feet across, but never even scratched the buildings on all four sides. The *éclat* appeared to have been shot high in air, and fallen harmlessly to the ground some distance away. Bouy is certainly a poor place for a hospital. Besides the big aviation field, it contains a good sized munition depot, and since it is liable to continual bombardment the authorities decided to evacuate all their patients to St. Hilare, even though the shelling was over. We worked at this for several hours, along with a French section. We formed in a long line at the H.O.E. in St. Hilare, waiting for the bulky French ambulances, which had arrived before us, to discharge their *blessés*.

It was a very hot day and the air inside the ambulances was stifling. I gave my two Algerians a sip of water from my canteen, and they were so delighted with it, that I carried it down the line. Finally I came to

1. An admiring group of officers gathered around Guynemer, the peer of all aviators who was killed September, 1917, just after downing his 5ard adversary.
2. An American tractor, used for hauling big guns, being carried to the front.
3. A German aeroplane bomb, exploding in front of a French aerodrome.

1. The mill at St. Etienne au temple which the Boches destroyed in 1914, during the Battle of the Marne.
2. Eighty years old and doing her bit in the garden.
3. A group of Boche prisoners. The man in the centre is a stretcher bearer, and will have to be returned.

a couple of wounded Boches, who couldn't resist the temptation of *"Ein trinken Wasser,"* although at first they thought it was poisoned. The average German prisoner I have seen so far has been an ill-fed, stupid-looking, round-headed specimen who looked mighty sick of the war. But these fellows, although rather thin, had bright, intelligent faces. One was nineteen, another twenty, and the third a little fellow who claimed to be twenty-four. I had a long talk with them, while we were waiting, although my own German was pretty well mixed with French words which slipped in unconsciously. They told me they had been shoved into the trenches, near Moronvilliers three days before, along with thousands of other troops in an attempt to check a big French attack, and had been captured when we advanced.

When I asked them what they thought of the *Kaiser* one shrugged his shoulders but the youngest boy said that Wilhelm was all right and claimed that he was really a peaceful soul. He added that the militaristic ministry was the source of most of their troubles. Concerning the cause of the war, they had the peculiar idea that Russia had unexpectedly attacked them in 1914, and they had been forced to resist. When I questioned them about food, they said they had been getting plenty of meat all spring, but that they had very little bread and scarcely any potatoes. The attacking divisions get better food than any other. They told me our entry into the war was a great shock to the German people, and they could see no reason for our doing so. With the Allies backed by our strength now, they didn't think they would win the war, but supposed it would soon end in a draw. They are sure they won't be forced to accept our terms, however. I got a few buttons, from them before I left, as souvenirs.

There were two German aviators next to these Algerians who had been brought down by Guynemer from about twelve thousand feet. Their machine had turned over again and again in their fall but they managed to catch themselves a few hundred feet from the ground. Of course they landed with terrific force anyway; but luckily right side up, and now, although their skin has turned blue from the fall, and though the shock itself almost killed them, they will live.

*June 15th*, 1917.                                                                                            Recy.

This continued repos stuff is absolutely degrading. We won't be good for anything after the war. We do nothing except loaf, loaf, loaf all day long and perhaps once a week go to Vadenay or St. Hilare, for a few *malade* calls. Just for fun I have written an outline of all I did today, dividing it up according to hours. Here it is:

7:30—Breakfast gong, an old shell case, sounds and we pile out of our cars to the *salle à manger* for oatmeal and prune *confiture*.

8:00—All is well. Breakfast is now over and the poker crowd have started the day's game. The bridge fiends are playing behind Tenney's car and two fellows are shooting craps. Gilmore and I are matching pennies and Stanley is trying to feed a raw egg to our new mascot, a young red fox.

9:00—It is getting warmer. I have gone to my car and started a letter home.

9:15—It is much too hot to write. I have given up my letter for a book in French on artillery.

9:30—Artillery is dull, especially in French. I am now reading one of Ring Lardner's latest in the *Saturday Evening Post*.

10:30—It got so hot that I fell asleep on the last page of the story. Reading is too strenuous for me today.

11:00—I loafed, fooled around and monkeyed for half an hour. I spent part of this time in planning how to waste away the afternoon.

12:00—I took a picture a few minutes ago while sitting in my car. I could have gotten it much better if I had moved but it was too much trouble.

1:00—By dint of great effort Ott Kann and I covered the entire two hundred yards between the cantonment and the canal in a little less than twenty minutes and gazed upon the barges which are being towed along by man and woman power. Work like that would kill us (or do us a whole lot of good).

1:30—Mosquitoes and bugs pestered us too much by the water so we sauntered rapidly back to the quarters and watched the poker game for a while. They are out for an endurance record today, trying to beat the one of fourteen hours and eight minutes made at Ste. Menehould, when they played until Bob, the old waiter, brought in the "Quaker Oats" at breakfast.

3:30—I fell asleep about two o'clock while I was attempting to decide whether I would finish my letter home or start a new story.

4:30—When climbing out of my car I noticed that one of my tires was flat. I think I shall pump it tomorrow. Number One spark-plug is also on the blink, but there is no use changing it until I have to go out sometime in a hurry.

This is what we do every day. No one has any pep. I think I'll go crazy, if we don't get out of this soon.

*June 17th.* Recy.

Section Twelve is fast becoming the most religious of all the American sections at the front. It has its Sunday morning service in English with a Protestant minister from the French army in charge. A week ago Saturday one of the workmen in the artillery repair shop nearby, dropped around to the cantonment and suggested our having a service every Sunday. He had been preaching in England for some time when the war broke out and when he found he couldn't get in the army as a chaplain he enlisted in the artillery. For several Sundays now we have been gathering together in the *salle à manger* tent and with the aid of a hymn book and a Bible which I brought along we have gotten on splendidly. He preaches well, is very sincere, and makes really very few grammatical errors.

Sammy and I are trying to find a way to get to Reims before we go up to the front again. It is only twenty-five miles, but we don't seem to be able to work it. We wouldn't be allowed to take a car that far and since dawn to dusk is our limit for hikes during our days off duty, it is hardly possible in this time to walk fifty miles, and see the city itself. Moreover, the Boches have been punishing it severely lately. Yesterday they dropped in two thousand five hundred shells and the day before an even two thousand. This wouldn't keep us away, however, if we could find the means of quick transportation.

*June 19.* Vadenay.

I am on duty here for the second time. We are supposed to spend our twenty-four hours carrying *malades* suffering from indigestion and earache to the H. O. E. at St. Hilare. But luckily for us there are not many such cases and we spend most of our time in the village. We are the first Americans that have ever been in the place, at least since the war began. The woman at the *epicerie* almost embraced me this morning when I called to buy a pound of figs; and then she wanted to know if I didn't think the war would end right away, with us in it. She was actually so glad to see me that she put an orange in with the figs as a present.

There is a *saucisse* just behind the town and we watch it by the hour. It is attached to the ground by a thin wire cable which is reeled in and out at will upon a big steel drum. This is operated from an auto truck, designed especially for this purpose. And whenever the pilot thinks an enemy aviator is coming after him, he signals to those below; and they bring him in at a terrific rate. Sometimes he comes down so fast he appears to be falling. The pilot whom we saw killed near Dombasle last March would not have lost his balloon and incidentally his life if they had started to bring him down at full speed before the Boche was upon him.

I thought, as I lay on my stretcher last night and the dull echoes of the distant *tir de barrage* in the Mont Cornillet Sector were gradually putting me to sleep, "would one year from today see France in civilian clothes again; and when twelve months had passed would No Man's Land be under cultivation once more?" I wonder if it will.

*June 25th.*  Still at Recy.

The *brancardiers* think that we are soon going to move to Suippes or some place near there. If this rumours is true it will mean a lot of hard work for us. I am afraid, however, it won't last very long for me personally. For my time expires on the eighth of July and I will very likely leave the section then. I am expecting a cable from home, telling me whether or not I can enter Aviation or go down to Salonika in the Ambulance Service there. If the family disapproves of both of these things, I presume that I shall have to go home.

There is a little mouse who lives in the wall of our dining-room whom we have nicknamed Napoleon Xenophon. He is a master of strategy and the combined efforts of the entire section have not yet resulted in his capture. Harrison and Tenney formulated the brilliant scheme yesterday of placing a string noose over the mouth of his home; and patiently waiting, one on either side, until the villain should emerge, they intended to jerk the cord and crush in his neck from the terrific pressure. But although they stayed there for several hours and got him to come out quite frequently by using bread for bait (something an American mouse would turn up his nose at) the clever little animal never waited long enough in the noose for them to pull it shut. Several times it seized the bread and returned to its hole before they could jerk the string. And at last, when they were really developing some speed with their trap, the mouse appeared at a side entrance to his home and laughed at them.

The 221st had a big entertainment last evening in the town hall. The big event of the evening was a boxing match between a French middleweight and Kid Crowhurst of the American Ambulance. They fought on a tiny platform not more than ten feet square, and our veteran mechanic almost broke up the performance when a clean right hook from his mighty arm sent his opponent sprawling onto a chair off stage, on which lay the violin of the musician who came next on the program. The instrument was ruined; and although the audience didn't object at all, the fight was stopped in the next round.

Mike O'Connor, one of the new men, and I walked into Châlons the other morning. He stopped at the Hospital "*Militaire*" to consult a doctor about something. While I was waiting for him outside I got into conversation with one of the patients, a young fellow not over eighteen, who I learned was a second lieutenant in the artillery. He had studied at Fontainebleau and had been wounded about two weeks ago, during the big offensive near Auberive and Moronvilliers. He spoke English well and told me all about himself and his family. He lives on the Rue Boissiere in Paris, only a short distance from Rue Raynouard. His captain told him before he left that he would be cited, so that he will very likely get his *Croix de Guerre*. I had to leave him when O'Connor came out; but I promised to call again and also to look him up in Paris, since there is a chance that he may be home on furlough when I come in the eighth of July.

Tenney, Harrison and Sinclair left the section today. They are going to join Section Ten now in Albania.

*June 27th*, 1917. Recy, yet.

Sammy Lloyd and I hiked about twenty miles yesterday. We rode with Craig as far as Bouy and then went a-foot towards Mourmelon le Petit where Section Fourteen is quartered. (Sammy came over on the *Chicago* with a number of their men.) We walked along an old Roman road for a while and passed the monument commemorating the defeat of Attila and the Huns. It seemed rather a coincidence that sixteen hundred years later the same Huns are being again defeated within a few miles of the spot.

We arrived at Mourmelon at three o'clock and the fellows there were kind enough to take us out to their posts, when they changed shifts two hours later. They go through Prosnes which is a badly wrecked place, and they have two little stations called Constantine and Moscow at the foot of Mont Cornillet and Mont Haut. They have had some hot times here. Even today the last part of the road had a number of fresh shell holes. Near their *abri* I photographed some dead Boches which the French have not had time to bury yet.

The odour there was frightful. One of the fellows who had been on duty said that a German shell had fallen among the bodies during the night and mangled them more than ever. He also told us of the new use which the Germans have for their dead. Instead of burying them, a process which is expensive and certainly very inefficient, they collect several thousand bodies, load them onto freight cars and take them to a factory some distance behind the lines. Here they are put into a big machine like a sausage grinder and when the residue has been chemically treated they are able to extract a considerable amount of glycerine from it.

This of course is very valuable to them in the manufacture of high explosives. The dead men are all supposed to be very patriotic and probably nothing pleases them more than to look down (or up, I don't know which) from their new homes and see that they have helped the Fatherland to the end. We were not able to stay here very long; we had to go back on the car returning to Mourmelon. And after eating supper with their section there, we set out on our long journey to Recy. Sammy took with him a German machine gun belt containing five hundred bullets which one of Fourteen's men sold him. We couldn't walk very fast with it and didn't get home until midnight.

About ten of us rode up to the Russian Hospital near Mourmelon le Grand this morning to attend the funeral of Paul Osborne, the Section Twenty-eight man who was killed near Prosnes a few days ago. A protestant army chaplain, the only one I have seen in France, paid the last tribute over his body. They buried him with military honours. Old Glory was draped over the coffin, and his coat with the *Croix de Guerre* which they had given him, was placed upon it. We marched away before the body was lowered into the grave, as is the custom at such funerals.

*June 30,* 1917.                                         Ferme de Piemont.

We packed up our belongings this morning, threw the heavy stuff into the white truck and the G. M. C., and the rest in the ambulances, and bade Recy a joyful farewell. One o'clock found the whole convoy in our new cantonment at Ferme de Piemont, three miles south of Suippes. We are relieving Section Eight. They have been here seven weeks and gone through some very interesting work but no real big attacks. Tomorrow we take over their posts and they go back to Dommartin or Châlons with their division. There are four front line posts, Pont Suippes, Jonchery, Bois Carré and Ferme de Wacques, and a relay

1. Getting the village children ready for a photograph. The little fellow in the centre is holding the pup "Montzèville," our section mascot.
2. Both eyes out and both arms torn to pieces by shellsplinters.
3. A. Piatt Andrew, director of the Field Service and Major Church, U. S. A., visiting our section in Champagne.

1. THE FRENCH SAUSAGE OR OBSERVATION BALLOON. THE SMALL BAGS IN THE REAR ACT AS RUDDERS, AND KEEP THE BALLOON ALWAYS WITH THE WIND.
2. SOLDIERS UNLOADING CYLINDERS OF HYDROGEN, USED TO INFLATE THE BALLOON.
3. THE GREAT MOTOR TRUCK AND STEEL DRUM WHICH REELS IN THE 7000 FEET OF THIN WIRE CABLE BY WHICH THE BALLOON IS RAISED AND LOWERED.

at both Suippes and Cuperly. Besides this, three cars are always on call at the cantonment. This means ten fellows a day for the work and consequently twenty-four hours on duty and twenty hours off, for every man.

From the woods behind the quarters we can see Mont Cornillet, Mont Haut and the ridge above Moronvilliers, a few miles northwest of us. Our division will not be on the hill at all but will occupy the trenches from Auberive, at its foot, to a point near Souain and Ferme de Navarin. This means eight thousand troops holding a front of less than two miles.

*July 1st.*                              *Abri* at Ferme de Wacques.

Once more at a post, once again waiting for *blessés* with old 464. I arrived at seven this morning, relieved the Section Eight man who was here and as soon as he had gone I chased over to the *brancardiers' abri* for a bite to eat. But alas, their supplies had been delayed somewhere on the road and they didn't expect them before night. This wasn't a very bright outlook for the day, with nothing to eat until suppertime. Luckily I had a loaf of bread in the side-box of my car and by breaking it into small pieces and calling each one by a different name such as creamed potatoes, waffles, salad and *bisque* ice-cream, I had two very enjoyable meals on the front seat of my ambulance.

The general of the Seventy-first Division came here in his staff car very early this morning, for a promenade in the trenches. I talked with his chauffeur for a few minutes and learned that he does this every day, in order to keep in touch with his men. Later on, since there was not a sign of a *blessé*, I strolled off towards the *"premières lignes"* But I stumbled across a battery of "75's" before I had gone very far and found a young *"aspirant"* (cadet) there named Lucot. When he learned that I was an American, he was just as anxious to talk to me as I was curious to examine the battery. He took me around to the officers' *abri* and introduced me to his captain and two lieutenants. After they had shown me several of the guns and carefully explained the mechanism of each and also of the machine which sets the time-fuses, they took me down into the deep munition dugouts where they pointed with great pleasure to a number of American made shells.

Then they did something entirely unexpected. They invited me into dinner. I knew this would be a thousand times better than my menu of army bread, and since there was very little chance of *blessés* arriving at the post for two or three hours, I accepted at once. The meal was served in the captain's *abri*, with ten feet of carefully laid earth and logs between us and any Boche shells which might break outside. I was kept pretty busy through it all, trying to eat and answer their countless questions. They wanted to know how many troops we had in France, if our men would actually get into the trenches this fall, if their "75" wasn't better than our American three- inch gun and of course a lot of things about the Ambulance Service. When I had a chance I would question them about French and German time fuses or perhaps the range of different guns: but I didn't have many opportunities to do this. Very often throughout the meal, we touched our glasses and drank the health of the "*capitaine*" or some other member of the party; and, as usually happens over here, the last toast was to "the speedy ending of the war."

After lunch they told me they wanted some bright American girls for their *marraines*. So I wrote down the names and addresses of four of my friends at home whom I thought would be willing to correspond with them. Then I described each one in turn and let each officer pick the one he wanted. It was very funny the way they debated about the girls. They decided that Lucot should take the youngest, who was very intelligent and quite small, because he also was young and small, although he didn't come up to the intelligence standard; the captain preferred the tall and sedate brunette because his grandmother was tall and sedate. The lieutenants had a terrible dispute over the remaining two, one of whom was a marvellous dancer and the other very beautiful. They ended the argument at last by throwing up a two-*franc* piece and calling the pretty girl heads and the dancer tails.

After dinner, Lucot showed me the road which the *ravitaillement* wagons use at night when they go up to the second and third line trenches. I don't believe the road to Esnes itself was ever in such terrible condition. As far as you could see it wound on with little holes, medium sized holes and real "420s" everywhere. It is just about like walking from one hole to another. Occasionally when we would come to one of the really big ones, there wouldn't be any road at all, only a great crater thirty feet across and easily fifteen deep.

I was obliged to return to the post at two o'clock and Lucot was kind enough to walk back with me. On the way I took a few photographs of a big mine which exploded in March 1915 when the French made a three-mile advance here. We walked all through the former Boche trenches and the old "No Man's Land" which is only a couple of hundred yards from the battery. Our conversation was very peculiar, for everything he said was in English, which he had studied for five years, and I answered him in French, as well as I could.

There were no *blessés* during the afternoon but I stuck pretty close to the post on account of the rather long time I had spent at the battery. I am writing by my petrol lamp in the *brancardiers' abri*.

*July 4th*, 1917.                                                      Post at Jonchery.

Everybody in the section is hopping mad. Here's the biggest celebration of the year coming off in Paris today. The first of our troops to arrive in France will parade and the whole city will be wild with joy; and they won't allow a single one of us even a forty-eight-hour furlough to see it. All the other sections are sending in ten or twelve men apiece but we will have to fool around out here and be satisfied with a bottle of champagne apiece, and an omelette for breakfast. I won't even get this, for I am on duty here at Jonchery while the rest are having the treat at the cantonment in Ferme de Piemont.

This post is a relay on the way to Pont Suippes and is worked in the same manner as Esnes and Montzèville used to be. I started out at the former yesterday morning and have gone back and forth many times since then. At Pont Suippes we have to leave our cars in one particular place or they will be spotted by one of the dozen German sausages which are busy from dawn till dusk just across the lines.

One of the generals' chauffeurs stopped his machine recently in an unprotected place near the bridge and while waiting there alone was killed by a balloon-directed shell. The Frenchmen showed me where it all happened. Afterwards, I bickered with them for a lot of time-fuses which they had dug up from some neighbouring shell holes. I gave one fellow a dollar Ingersoll watch for five perfect fuses, including two aluminium ones for which he had been obliged to dig down four feet into the earth. While we were bargaining, a *brancardier* came towards us with a huge eel which he had caught in the stream of "Suippes." He skinned it in the *abri*, and we had "*eel à la tranchée*" for lunch. It wasn't a bit bad.

While I was taking a few snapshots of the shell holes around the *abri* and in the little cemetery across the road, I ran across a young artillery lieutenant. I could see that he hadn't been out of Fontainebleau long and I thought perchance he might know Lucot or Bernard Lar Lenque, both of whom studied there last year. He let out a great yell when I mentioned the latter's name, and seizing my hand, told me that Bernard was his cousin. His own name was Christian Thurneyssen. Of course he wanted to know all about him, where I had met him and how he was getting along. Only the day before he had learned that Bernard had been wounded. We had a long talk together, and in the end I promised to look up his family when I went into Paris.

I will probably leave the section next week. Consequently I am gathering a lot of souvenirs to take back home with me. Gilmore said the fine lot he lugged all the way back to Italy with him, when he was on his permission, was not appreciated by his family. He had thought they would go wild over the fuses and helmets but they hardly looked at them. There was some excuse for them, however, because they had been seeing things like these ever since Italy entered the war. I think it will be different in America; anyway, I am taking back a couple of hundred pounds of junk. This evening I added a Boche canteen, a common soldier's flashlight and one of their trench knives to my collection. I got them from a *poilu* who didn't want to give them up at all, because his permission was coming soon; but when I explained how interested the people in America would be in them and parted with my fountain pen, a compass and one of my many Ingersoll watches, to help with the persuasion, he yielded.

Last night I watched the *tir de barrage* of a German attack and I was happy. A terrific bombardment started just an hour ago a couple miles north of us and the sky overhead was made brilliant by bursting shells. Then several of our own nearby batteries began hammering away in answer to the red fire "Artillery Wanted" signals sent up from the first line trenches; and gradually every available gun along our front got into action. From all sides came the glare from the mouths of busy seventy-fives. And with it all were the star-light shells which broke forth behind the curtain of fire and showed to us, as we stood upon the sand-bags over the *abri*, a great wall of smoke. Now and then, when a slight lull came between the roar of the shells, we could hear the familiar rat-tat-tat of the machine guns. The thing kept increasing in volume until every battery was going to its limit; and as I watched it, I pictured the first line trenches turned into inferno: and I was glad I was not there.

I had a few hours sleep afterwards in a stuffy little underground room where six of the *brancardiers* bunk. But they called me out at midnight when the *blessés* from the attack began to come in. After three or four runs to Suippes I ended up here at Jonchery at five this morning. But instead of going to bed as I should have, I spent an hour trying to chip off the compression of a Boche "210" which had fallen

1. RESERVE SOLDIERS, FORTY TO FIFTY YEARS OLD, ARRANGING AND TAKING INVENTORY OF A PILE OF 12 INCH SHELLS.
2. THE TWO HUSKIEST WORKMEN IN THE CROWD LIFTING ONE OF THE 450 LB. SHELLS.
3. AN ARTILLERYMAN PUTTING A TIME SHELL INTO THE BREECH OF AN ANTI-AIRCRAFT "75," WHICH, ALTHOUGH MOUNTED ON AN AUTOMOBILE, FIRES TWENTY-EIGHT SHOTS A MINUTE.

1. The famous hanging clock in the ruined church at St. Hilare le Grand.
2. The fallen bells and the praying angels in the church at Suippes. The whole steeple has been shot away.
3. One hundred *poilu* graves, each marked with a little tricolour tin target and *"Mort pour la France."*

near my car. It had certainly been put on to stay, for I broke my Ford screw-driver prying on it. I had to be satisfied with a mere six inch piece because my monkey wrench which was the only tool left that might have worked, wouldn't fit into the groove. . . .

I had breakfast with the undertakers who are the only people besides ourselves in the village. There are no *brancardiers* here since it is a relay station; and so we eat with them. They are a queer lot, simply four old soldiers who can't fight any more, who have been detailed to bury all the dead from one of our regiments, the Two Hundred and Twenty-first. They showed me the record which they keep of the bodies and it contained the names of twenty soldiers who have been killed during the six days the division has been in the trenches. I had no idea that the mortality would be so low along an average front like Champagne at the present time. For this means less than one man in ten killed in a whole year of fighting. I told them that I was going back to America soon and they gave me, to take along a souvenir, one of the little red, white and blue targets which are placed on the grave of every French soldier.

The town seems to have received two very heavy bombardments since the war began. While I was wandering around taking pictures, after I left the members of the cemetery department, I came across a house, not so badly wrecked as the others, from which, if I climbed up onto the roof, I thought I might get a good view of the trenches. The stairs leading up to the second floor had been shot away; and as I was hunting for some projecting timber by which I might pull myself up, my eyes fell upon two inscriptions scrawled upon the plaster. The first one said that five people, probably those who had been living in the house, had been killed here in March, 1915. And from the one below it, I gathered that three soldiers who had been passing through the village and had stopped in the house over night, had lost their lives in a bombardment in July, 1916. . . . I went upstairs afterwards and was surprised to find a crop of hay growing in the front bedroom. Then I climbed up on the roof and took several photographs of Mont Haut when a lot of shells were breaking upon its summit.

I got another rather interesting picture during the morning. This was of the church in St. Hilare le Grand, between here and Pont Suippes. Most of the steeple has been shot away but the old clock is still hanging there, suspended only by the cement on one side. We know the exact time the building was shelled, for the hands point to half-past one.

My twenty-four hours were up an hour ago, and no one has come to relieve me as yet. I can't complain though, for I would be late too, if I were having a good breakfast.

*July 6th.*                                              Tirage at Suippes.

Mike O'Connor and I have been out here all day and only had one run apiece. The post here is a "*tirage*" where all the *blessés* from the other posts are left and then taken by the men on duty there to the hospitals at Cuperly and St. Hilare au Temple. If these become overcrowded they are sent on to base hospitals at Châlons or Bar-le-Duc; and from there any cases which require special attention or a long period of recuperation are sent into Paris by train. Like all the other towns near the front, Suippes has been shelled considerably and occasionally even now the Boches drop in a few *obus*. They take particular delight in banging away at the railroad station, for though the inhabitants have been forced to leave the village, all the military supplies for this sector are brought up here by train. A *poilu* was killed here only yesterday by a "210."

Mike and I got permission for a few minutes off about noon. We walked over to the church which was unharmed, with the exception of the belfry which had been torn away. The four bells were lying where they fell, in front of the altar, and the statues of two angels, kneeling in prayer, stood behind them. It was such an odd scene that I took several photos of it. Then we found some *poilus* who had a number of vases they had painstakingly hammered out from brass shell casings. I gave one of my Ingersolls for a pair of seventy-fives, decorated with a sort of grape-vine design, and five *francs* for four cute little "37" vases. Then we each bought a *briquet*, modelled after the French army canteen and exceedingly well put together. They told us it took a whole week to make one; but it keeps them busy during those periods, when they almost go crazy from the mo- notony of the life.

There is a large field between here and Ferme de Piemont where they have machine-gun and hand-grenade practice. Stanley, Sammy Lloyd and myself walked there last Sunday and looked the place over. We got into conversation with some soldiers and soon they were telling us how to throw hand-grenades. We claimed that the American method, the baseball way, was much better and proved it by hurling one of the cast iron bombs about the size of a lemon, fully fifty feet farther than their best mark. But they explained and rightly enough, too, that their over-arm method never tires one very much; whereas ours does, after very few throws.

*July 8th.*         Cantonment at Ferme de Piemont.

Since our arrival here I have been aching to visit the captured Boche trenches near Auberive which the French took in their recent Champagne offensive. And so when I learned from "Chef" Coan, after I came in yesterday, that I wouldn't be on duty at Bois Carré or Pont Suippes again before I left the section, I arranged matters so that Mike O'Connor and I could start out early and bum around for three or four hours before it was time for the other car to come in. We left the cantonment at four this morning, missed a couple of shells rather nicely near the Mourmelon fork and arrived at Bois Carré just as the first German sausage was popping up over the horizon.

I intended to head for Auberive which is about a mile from the post and although now in French hands is nevertheless only a few hundred yards from the present lines. But somehow we got into the wrong *boyau* and wandered several miles out of our way before we realized where we were. We had to give up the Auberive scheme altogether and go north towards Moronvilliers. But there was no direct route to the old German lines here and we were obliged to crawl through a lot of unfinished trenches and others blocked with barbed-wire. Finally it got so bad we were forced into the open for several hundred yards. This would have been quite safe a mile behind the front lines at La Harazee, where it is very hilly; but in this flat country you can be seen two or three miles away, and at one mile you are taking somewhat of a chance.

It was exactly an hour and a half after we left Bois Carré that we saw the first sign of old German occupation. This was a large pile of hand-grenades which were unmistakably Boche. Then came an *abri* with "*Sicherheit hier*" written on one of the timbers and I noticed that it was quite carefully built. It occurred to me as I read the words, how strange it was that the people of Goethe's race should be our enemies in a war like this. Now we ran into an old supply station where barbed-wire, shells and trench torpedoes lay scattered around. Across from this, but still in the trench, was a grave, marked by a simple wooden cross. And I noticed that the name inscribed upon it was German and that he belonged to the foreign legion of the French Army. They lost a good many thousand men when they took Mont Cornillet and Mont Haut here.

I picked up a Boche helmet a little farther on; the wearer had been killed by a shell splinter which penetrated the steel. The blood had rusted it and we could see traces of it quite plainly. Unfortunately we had to return to the post before eight-thirty so we had very little time there. We took as many souvenirs as we could carry, including two unexploded torpedoes and an Austrian "88." Just as we were leaving, we asked one of the *poilus* who was at work putting the trenches into shape once more, if he had seen any "77" cartridge cases lying about. And instead of giving us an empty one, what did he do but pick up a whole loaded shell and slam it against the side of the trench until it came apart. Then he dumped all the powder out on the ground and gave us the casing.

On our way back we had a close call. We had gone only a short distance when we found we were heading straight for a battery which the Boches were shelling. There was no other way to the post except by a long detour; so we decided to chance it, figuring that we could get past in the four minute interval at which the shells seemed to be coming. But we weren't quite quick enough and a big fellow burst about seventy-five yards away just as we got there. Éclat shot by us and over our heads and a few seconds later twigs and small branches from the nearby trees began to patter down around us. We didn't stop here, not even long enough to take a picture. As soon as we arrived at the post we dumped the souvenirs into the rear of Frutiger's car. I was to ride back to Ferme de Piemont with him and he left shortly afterwards.

Like some of the *poilus*, we have the craze for unloading everything we think would make a good souvenir. Every day somebody brings in a hand-grenade or a new kind of fuse and there is always somebody foolish enough to monkey with it. I suppose we have carried five or six *poilus* already, wounded as they were taking something apart and yet we go right ahead with it.

Today Payne offered Frazer the revolver which he borrowed from the little armoury in the barn at Suippes if the latter would unload his big Boche torpedo. And although he had only two days more to spend in the section and didn't know a single thing about the construction of the affair, since it was German, he put it in a vice in the tool-room, and took it apart with a pipe-wrench. It could have gone off just as well as not and he wouldn't have been any the wiser. It doesn't wound like a hand grenade, it kills.

## German Trench Torpedo

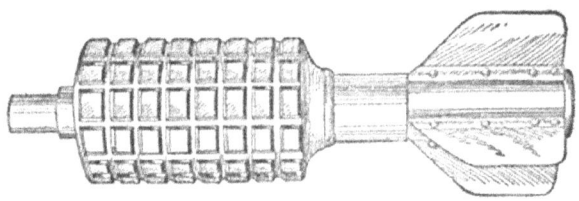

The base is made of iron, so moulded that the torpedo will break up into 98 squares. It can be shot either from a gun or catapult. It is exploded when the percussion cap on the extreme right strikes the ground. The tin rudders in the rear keep it from turning over in the air.

This is the same torpedo, the unloading which is described in the diary of July 8, 1917. Although this particular type weighs only five or six pounds, there are some in use which are one hundred times as heavy.

*July 9th*, 1917.                                    Ferme de Plemont.

It's a true saying that a Ford will run anywhere you take it. Frutiger ran his machine into a tree on the Suippes road, but instead of climbing it as the Ford joke-book would have it, the car bounded over to the opposite side of the road and laid there for several minutes on its back with the rear wheels spinning around at a great rate, before he was able to shut off the motor. Then he waited until a couple of Frenchmen came along and with their help turned it right side up again. After this he thanked them and rode off as though nothing had happened.

Sammy Lloyd told me some time ago of the munition depot over the hill, and so this morning we took our cameras and walked up there. About twenty soldiers were working on a pile of twelve inch shells ("280's") when we arrived, arranging them in long rows and covering them afterwards with a sort of pine-bough camouflage. They thought it fine to have their pictures taken; and I got the two strongest men in the crowd to lift one of the big projectiles for me while I took the photograph. They managed to hold it up several seconds although it weighs four hundred and fifty pounds. Then their sergeant showed us the whole depot, and told us that although they had 50,000 shells stored there, they were so carefully concealed that the Boche aviators couldn't tell them from common underbrush.

*July 11,* 1917.   My last day with good old Section Twelve.

Benney and I left the section for good today. He goes to Avord to enter the Aviation School and I am going home by way of England. I'd a thousand times rather stay in France until the war's over but the family doesn't agree with me. Both of the last two cables from America read "Home." Therefore I must go home to argue it out. We have been packing most of the morning and getting our souvenirs so mixed with our clothes that they don't look suspicious. I have two hundred and sixty pounds of stuff which I hope I can get in all right. We are waiting for the *camionette* now to come and take us into Châlons. I have finished saying goodbye to the fellows and have just snapped a last picture of a group of them together in front of Ray William's car, smoking their good old Bull Durham. As for old 464, I patted her radiator in a last fond caress and gave her a final drink of water five minutes ago. Dear old "Shen-ick-a-day-dy," as the *poilus* call her.

CHAPTER 5

# Coming Back

*July 14th.*                               5 Rue Le Kain, Pans.

Paris is wonderful now, far prettier than before, and I hate to think of leaving next Saturday. But I have decided to go to England with two ambulance fellows, Anderson and Lillie, and spend two or three weeks there. Then I shall sail from Liverpool and get home about the middle of August. I tried to get some information concerning the army transports and the possibility of shipping home on one. None of the army officers, however, could tell me anything about the dates and arrivals of ships, excepting that St. Nazaire was one of the ports. If my funds run low in England, I may be obliged to return to France and take passage home this way. I spent the whole morning yesterday trying to get my passport *viséd* by the numerous officials, such as the police and consuls, so that I might leave France. At one place they told me I couldn't go to England at all, but I didn't bother with them. I went to the British Permit office and found that I could. I was all ready to go, after a few hours chasing around, while a young English governess whom I met at the *Prefecture* of Police told me she had been waiting three months to have her papers approved and hadn't received them yet.

You can't help spending money in Paris. Besides the usual little items such as *cafés*, opera and expensive meals, you want to buy everything you see. I have just paid out two hundred and ten *francs* for a new uniform for use in England, and one hundred and fifty more for a few little Parisian trinkets to take back to the family. Dinner last evening with Anderson cost me forty alone, and some films and printing paper at Kodaks, brought this up to ninety. Every time I change a one-hundred-*franc* note I see my chances as a first-class passenger on the trip home getting smaller and smaller.

Bernard Larlenque, the young artillery officer whom I met in the hospital at Châlons last month, is now in Paris. We went down together to the Avenue St. Germain early this morning to see the great "Independence Day" parade. I had heard about it before but I never imagined that it was such a big event. Fully fifty thousand troops marched by, the banner regiments of the French army. Everyone was happy, childishly happy, from the tiniest spectator who cheered with all his might to the soldiers themselves who brandished bouquets from their bayonets. When one of the crack *"chasseur"* companies was passing us, a handsome young woman darted forth from her place among the onlookers and gave a little bunch of roses to the captain leading them. He took the flowers, stooped and kissed her, and then marched on amid the deafening applause of the crowd. Shortly after this I got a fine close-up picture of General G———, one of the most famous *chasseur* generals, who dismounted from his horse to shake hands with a few wounded Algerians standing beside us on crutches, when the whole parade had stopped for a moment.

I took dinner with Bernard afterwards at his home near the Étoile and spent several hours with his charming family. His father is a captain in the artillery, his seventeen-year-old brother leaves for the front next month, and the one, fourteen, a boy scout, is working on a farm. None of these were present when I was there, but I saw the three younger children with their mother, who is most attractive.

*July 18.* Paris still

I have had a pretty full program since the day of the parade. Sunday I dined again at the Larlenque's and afterwards Bernard and I promenaded on the Avenue Bois de Boulogne. There were uniforms of all the allied armies, even a few American scattered in the throng. Afterwards we called on the Thurneyssens, the parents of the aspirant whom I met at Pont Suippes. I left with them some pictures I had taken of him at the front. I stood there like a perfect dummy when Bernard introduced me to the *Madame*, for I discovered for the first time I didn't know a single word of polite-society French. I almost let slip the *poilu* equivalent for "glad to know you, old chap," but it dawned on me that I was in Paris, not at the front, and I kept silent. Showing her the photographs, however, started the ball rolling and I had no trouble after that.

Even the French are crazy about Charlie Chaplin. Barney Faith

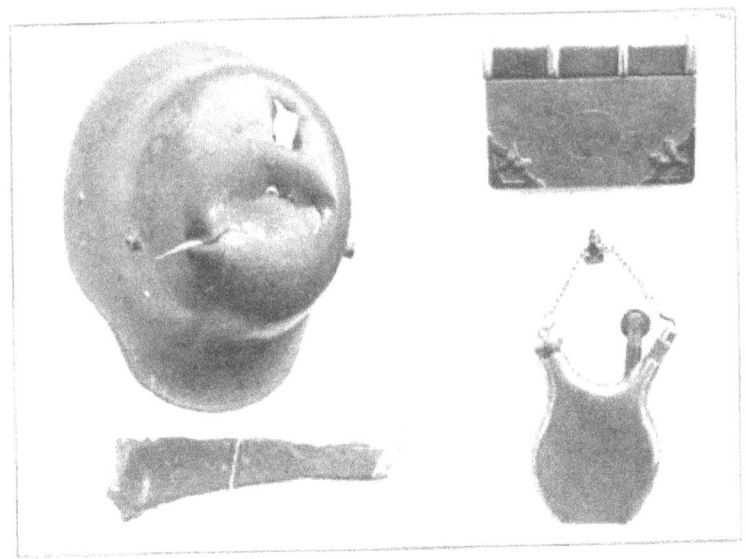

1. A German helmet which the author found near Auberive in Champagne. The soldier wearing it was instantly killed by a large piece of shell similar to the one shown below. The inside is covered with blood. It is interesting to note that this helmet is of tempered steel and can resist two or three times as much pressure as the French or American. A "32" revolver bullet fired at twenty feet, made no impression on the German helmet, while a similar shot pierced the front and back of a French helmet.
2. Two types of briquets—cigarette lighters. Both these were carefully hammered out by poilus "*en repos*" from bits of copper compression bands and brass shell casings. The wick, concealed the cap on the right (lower picture), is fed by gasoline within the briquet.

1. A pill box or German machine gun post, made of solid concrete. In daytime the slits are covered with burlap sacking.
2. The entrance to another German machine gun post. The roof is composed of two feet of steel rails, corrugated iron and heavy timbers.
3. J.T. Lloyd of Cornell in a "210" shell hole. The Boches, firing from 12 miles away, missed the railroad tracks (in the background) at which they were firing, by ten feet.

and I saw him in *The Vagabond* at the Passy *Cinema* this evening!

Just as I am leaving, the front gets active again. Mont Cornillet is seeing some very heavy artillery fire once more and the French are launching a big attack at Hill 304. We have had more men killed in the last month than in the whole history of the Service. Craig, of Section Two, was hit by shell *éclat* near Dombasle and died a few hours later. A bomb from a German aeroplane got Norton of Section One yesterday, and Gailey and Hamilton were mortally wounded near Soissons last week. Then there were several other cases I have forgotten: and of course, Osborne of Twenty-eight, whose funeral we attended at Mourmelon.

Anderson, Lillie and I leave for London tomorrow morning; Lillie, to rest up after eight months with Section Ten in Albania, and Anderson, for his furlough.

*July 23.*                         Regent Palace Hotel, London.

We had an uneventful Channel trip from Havre to Southampton escorted by three British destroyers and zigzagging the entire distance. We had no trouble at either port, fortunately, and went up to London on the next train. We chose the Regent Palace in Piccadilly as our hotel because it had been recommended as the place where all "officers" back from France spent their permissions.

Ever since we arrived, we have been on the go. Sometimes it's sightseeing, and again it is shopping, and every evening we try the theatres. Last night we saw the *Maid of the Mountains*, and the day before, *Inside the Lines*. There are far more amusement places open here than in Paris, and a good many more civilians. The people seem happier I suppose because they have not had the war brought as close to them as the French. Early Sunday morning the "Air Raid" alarms sounded all over the city and everyone rushed outside to get a better view of the enemy's planes, instead of going down into the cellar as the officials expect them to do.

Several days ago I found a place called the "Indian Restaurant." Never thinking that this meant East instead of West Indian, I went in and ordered a meal. They brought me the queerest mess of food I have ever run across. And all of it, from the soup to the rice, was full of terrible curry. I finally gave it up and asked for some plain bread and butter. But they refused on the ground that I had already eaten the one piece which the food controllers allow at a meal. This scheme is really far more effective than the two wheatless days a week which they first tried. For it cuts down the use of white bread more than half, whereas the other way means only a ten or fifteen *per cent* reduction.

We are saluted everywhere. Once in a while a Tommy gets suspicious and doesn't bother with us, but usually he gives us a real snappy one. It was a lot of fun answering him at first, but when you have to give a couple of thousand every day, it gets tiresome. Of course they think we are commissioned officers or they wouldn't look at us. Even some old veterans of the Crimean war were fooled the other day and I felt so cheap afterwards that I wanted to turn around and tell them what I was. But except for this, our uniforms are a great help. By their aid we managed to hire a Hupmobile for the whole day yesterday, when half a dozen places had told us it was impossible to rent a car on account of the great scarcity of gasoline. They said they didn't even have enough for themselves. We toured up to Cambridge in the morning, through a number of pretty little villages with *Mother Goose* names. It was rather exciting at times for neither Anderson nor I had driven a Hup before; besides, the sudden change from driving on the right hand side of the road to the left, which is the English way, was hard to get used to. Lillie showed us around the University; Pembroke, where he himself had studied, and Christ's, Trinity and Kings Colleges. The only students left are a few East Indians and some young boys. The majority of colleges have been taken over by the government for training schools. Lillie learned from his proctor that three of his intimate friends had been killed in the service and that practically everyone in the university had enlisted.

I'm spending my money even faster here than I did in Paris. I ordered two new suits and a snappy raincoat from a tailor in Southampton Row. I walked over to the British Museum while I was up there, but found it had been closed for over a year. Fully a dozen people had told me before I went there that it was still open like the French in Paris, Londoners don't know London's attractions.

*July 27th*, 1917.                    Halsway Manor, Somerset.

London was new and interesting and I liked it; but this is really England here. Cardiff lies across the channel, in Wales, and Bristol lies on one side of us and the old forest of Exmoor on the other. Then south of us is Cornwall, the land of King Arthur and of Jack-the-Giant-Killer. We're just outside of Crowcombe and the hills behind the house overlook the sea. I am visiting Mrs. Rowcliffe, an old friend of my mother's whom the family had told me about before I left home.

She and her husband have a wonderful estate here, with a quaint old manor, part of which was built in the thirteenth century.

When I came here, I intended to stay only one night, but this is the third day now, and I am still here. Everything is new to me, from the heather and the bracken on the hills behind the manor to the low thatched cottages and the people themselves. Then there is the age of all the buildings. To think of living in a house built seven hundred years ago! But there are landmarks far older than this. The carpenter who drove me up from Stogumber Station to the Rowcliffe's, showed me a crude circle on the hillside, the remains of a Roman encampment; and from there on we drove up a rocky little lane over which the Phoenicians used to carry their tin to the sea.

Out here you can't believe there's a war, it's all so quiet and peaceful. I have only seen one Tommy since I've been here and he was some distance off, down on the main road. But the young men are gone just the same, though the people don't talk about it. There are no slackers loafing around. The gardener's boy is at the front, they tell me, with the Royal Engineers, and the only son of Colonel Gordon, who lives by himself in the village now, after thirty years in India, has just been killed in aviation. Every week or two some sad news like this comes to the little place. They have only a few young fellows left.

*July 30.*                                                      Paris once more.

England turned out financially just as I thought it would. It ended with either cabling home for money (when I had received two hundred extra already), trying steerage from Liverpool, or the transport idea. I figured that the last, although perhaps a wild goose chase, would be much cheaper than either of the other ways and whatever happened, far more interesting. So here I am, back in Paris again and ready to leave in an hour for St. Nazaire. I got by the customs all right this morning in Havre, but arrived at the depot just as they closed the baggage car of the train; and, of course, I couldn't put on my steamer trunk and duffel bag. In great agony I watched it pull out, leaving me to a ten hour wait for the next through-train to Paris. It wasn't as much of a sacrifice as I thought it was going to be, for I managed to persuade the T. M. office here to give me a free ticket all the way to St. Nazaire, a distance of more than four hundred and fifty miles.

Later I had a fine game of billiards in the back room of an old hotel with a convalescent English captain. Being in France once more gave me the notion that everyone ought to speak French. I became quite angry with a Tommy guarding a freight yard entrance when I politely asked him, "*Ou est la Rue Cherbourg?*", and he looked at me with a blank expression on his face. We had a good laugh together when I discovered my mistake.

 I carted all my luggage in a taxi to the Gare du Quai d'Orsay this morning and afterwards went up to Rue Raynouard to say goodbye to the fellows. Williams, Dixon, Gilmore and Frutiger are in from our section, and a number of other men whom I met at the front, from other sections. One hundred and ten new men arrived last week and a hundred the week before. This rapid increase from the paltry fifteen who came last January on the Espagne has forced the Field Service additional quarters. Barracks are being erected all over the grounds and the annex at 5 Rue Le Kain is housing seventy or eighty more.

 I spent a few hours at 21 Rue Raynouard, where I got a couple of letters and some photos to take back to America for the fellows, and bade them all farewell. Then I darted around the corner to the little convent laundry near the cinema, burst in among the startled nuns, got the shirts and handkerchiefs I had left there before I left for England and took the Metro to the Place de l'Opera. A quick supper at Duvals with Henry Houston and then over to the Quai d'Orsay again. I am sitting in the train there now. It is due to leave in three minutes.

*August 2nd.*   On Board the Transport *Florence Luckenbach*, In the Basin at St. Nazaire.

 I arrived here at seven-thirty yesterday morning after sitting up all night from Paris. I left my baggage in the depot and started immediately for the docks to see how my prospects for a ride home looked. There was nothing in the first basin, but the watchman there told me there were a number of American transports further down. But alas, when I finally located them, the marines on guard wouldn't let me go near, to ask about a job for the trip. And the answer they gave me at the base office was even worse. It was impossible. They couldn't allow it. These were transports for army supplies, not for lugging back bankrupt ambulance drivers. A hot breakfast after this cheered me up a little and I tried to break through the marines again.

 This time I tackled another bunch, told a pathetic story and they let me through on the sly. The captain was not on board, but one of the quartermaster clerks was, and after I had told him all about myself, he said he would fix me up, even if I had to go as a stowaway. There was a good chance to work my passage, however, for the chief steward and the cook were in the city jail, and they needed an extra man. They had just taken on a big negro the day before as mess-boy and I was offered a similar job. I signed the articles before he could think twice, put my luggage on board with the ship's crane, and had it down in the poop that night, before they could fire me. He told me the captain would be back from Paris the next day and hinted that I exchange my cane and good looking uniform for a somewhat tougher costume, one more becoming to a mess-boy's position.

So when I appeared for work that evening in the pantry, I had on a rough khaki shirt and the old breeches I'd worn all the months at the front. The two other mess-boys gave me a hearty welcome; their work would be lighter now. They didn't let me do much because it was my first meal and they thought I had better get used to it slowly. I washed something like two hundred dishes, in a thick, pasty lot of water which they only change once a day, cleaned up the two mess rooms, and scrubbed the floor of the pantry afterwards. It is delightfully interesting work. I imagine two weeks of it will lead me to decide upon it as my life's occupation.

While I was working I learned a little about the boat and the men on it. It seems the most of them came over just for the novelty of going to France; they had had a rather disagreeable trip and now that they were finally in France they were only allowed to leave the boat on special permission. Even then they couldn't leave St. Nazaire, which is a little town and not too interesting. None of them knew more than a few words of French, but it was a simple matter getting what they wanted in their time off duty. As for the fellows in jail, they had been impudent and insulting to the officers and would probably be taken back to America in irons. They didn't know exactly when the boat was to sail, but told me confidentially, it wouldn't be more than a day or two, since only the flour and eight of the big guns remained to be unloaded. They had taken fourteen days to cross: and figuring on this, we will get home about the nineteenth of August. Jack Fenton, the quartermaster clerk who signed me up, said I could sleep on the settee in his cabin tonight. So I am tucked up on it now, with a port-hole above me instead of the canvas curtain on the rear of my ambulance.

*August 4th,* 1917.     On the Transport *Luckenbach,*
At sea.

I thought my game was up for sure when the captain came back yesterday. He had almost decided to take me when suddenly it entered his mind that the colonel of the Base wouldn't approve of it. So off he sent me to that gentleman, at whose very office I had had so abrupt a dismissal the day before. But Fenton went along with me and together we made them think that I was necessary for the safe return of the *Luckenbach*. I was so happy on the way back to the boat that I accosted a German road worker under an American guard, to see if I could get his little cap for a souvenir. But the old boy (he must have been forty-five) said: "*Ich wurde, aber es ist verboten*": and as one of his comrades explained, the French require them to wear the coat and cap of their uniforms, if they still have them, when they get out of the war zone. This forms a pretty good means of identification.

Late Sunday night the good news came that we were to sail early the next morning, and along with it, something not quite so encouraging. This was that two steamers had been sunk in the harbour outside the city; and another, whose water tight compartments had held, had barely been able to get to port. From the reports we got, one would have thought there was a squadron of submarines waiting for us. But orders are orders, and therefore at five this morning, with all fifty-seven of the crew on deck, we sailed down the Loire, through two or three locks, and out into the ocean.

In a way I am glad to be going home. Yet leaving now, when our troops are just arriving and when I could get into any branch of the service from aviation to artillery, merely to enter college, doesn't seem exactly right. But the family can't see it my way. My regular mess-boy duties have started now. I was up at four this morning, to make coffee for the engineers and the officer on the bridge. I'd never made the stuff before, but I dumped two or three cups of grounds into an old pot, stole some hot water from the cook's steam-chest and let it boil on the back of the stove while I fixed some toast to go along with it. They complimented me on it when I took it to them at five o'clock, said it was nice and soapy, and hoped someone else would make it the next time.

After this I washed the dishes from the midnight-lunch of the crew, and then started chamber-maiding the rooms. You not only have to make the beds carefully, fold the pyjamas and straighten out the clothes of some measly under-officer whom you wouldn't have for a gardener at home, but you must even scrub out his wash bowl and keep his brasses in good condition. I almost fell out of the port-hole today when one of the engineers suggested that I remove the tobacco

1. A PILE OF DEAD BOCHES SOUTH OF MT. CORNILLET. THEY ARE LYING IN THE HOT SUN, AND BEING EATEN UP BY THE FLIES. AFTER A BIG ATTACK IT IS OFTEN WEEKS BEFORE ALL THE DEAD CAN BE BURIED.
2. TWO GERMAN PRISONERS, SLEEPING ON A COUPLE OF TIES IN A BARBED-WIRE INCLOSURE, NEAR THE FRONT. THEY WILL SOON BE REMOVED FROM THE WAR ZONE.

A Coudron, double motored observation plane, flying in the clouds two miles above the communication trenches visible on the right.

stains that I had left on his *cuspidor*. Only a few of them are cranky like this, however. They treat me pretty well: and Marty, one of my partners, says we will make twenty or thirty dollars in tips if we keep their rooms shipshape. I figure I ought to clear fifty dollars on the trip, counting my salary, at forty-five dollars a month and board, which I signed for. A first class passage on the Cunard line would cost one hundred dollars at least, so I am earning one hundred fifty dollars just by two weeks of delightful work. When meal time comes around, Marty sets the mess room table and gets things ready in general around the pantry, while John, the head mess-boy, puts the officers' saloon in order. I bring all the food in from the kitchen, stuff it into the little steam table in the corner and then go into the stewards room to copy the menu. Yesterday I tried it in French, but it didn't prove a great success, for when I asked the captain if he would like *hors d'œuvres* for a starter to Sunday night's supper, he said, "Yes, he hadn't had any good vegetable soup for a long time."

Fenton can't keep me any longer on his settee: so he has found a place for me in the hole where the other mess-boys bunk. It's a little bit of a room, barely large enough for two. But they have rigged up a shelf for a bed which, although crude and too short for me, is better than the stretcher I used at the front. The only really unfortunate feature about the place is the terrible odour which seems to come through the wall behind my bed. Marty says they pulled away the boards twice on the way over, in hopes of finding some dead fish or rats; there was nothing there and still the smell comes. I think I will take to the deck if it gets any worse.

*August 9th.*                      The "Dead Rat Cabin"
                                           on the *Florence Luckenbach*.

We received an S. O. S. call on Monday from the *Campana*, one of the Standard Oil tankers. She had just been torpedoed in the Bay of Biscay, three hundred miles south of us. She went down in less than five minutes, the wireless operator said. An hour later we got "Submarine ten miles ahead" and this kept everybody interested until dinner time.

Two days ago the destroyer which had convoyed us thus far from St. Nazaire wigwagged over that we were now out of the war zone and that she would have to leave us here. An hour later, just as a little squall set up, she turned her prow eastward and left us to the mercy of the subs. Since then it's become rougher and rougher and now the old tub, ten or twelve feet higher out of the water anyway than when they came over loaded, is tossing about like a cork. Yesterday the log read only four knots an hour during the forenoon, and from eight to eleven o'clock this morning we only made two knots. If our speed were to continue to decrease at this rate, we'd be going back towards France by tomorrow.

The chief engineer, a jolly old Scotchman named Henderson, asked to see my pictures of the front today, and after we had spent some time looking at them, he took me down into the engine room and showed me the whole works. There are always one engineer and a couple of oilers below: but they don't have to work very hard. They burn crude oil instead of coal and thereby eliminate stoking.... About noon they had trouble with the big piston and had to stop the ship for two hours to fix it.

*August 13th*, 1917.                       On the *Luckenbach*
                                                  1200 miles to Nantucket.

I get along pretty well as mess-boy in the routine work, but now and then I pull some terrible "boner." I've carried dinner up to the captain's cabin when the wind was so strong I had to crawl up the stairs backwards, sitting for a moment on each step; and I have washed dishes when the roll of the boat almost threw them out of the sink into the rag in my hand; but this noon my luck changed. Knowles, the deposed first cook, was helping Mike in the kitchen. It was just five minutes before lunch and I had given him the soup tureen to fill, so that I could have it ready in the pantry. The stuff was boiling and I had barely lifted the full kettle off the floor when Marty came strutting past to get the key to the ice box, and knocked the whole pail out of my hand. Poor Knowles' feet happened to be in the way and were badly burned before we could pull off his socks, and rub flour and oil on them. He went to bed and I guess they can't use him anymore this trip.

Fenton showed me the payroll this afternoon. There are fifteen nationalities represented among the fifty-six men in the crew. It starts out with twelve Americans and ends up with one Hollander, one Pole and a Swiss. The latter is really French, I think; at least he knows Paris pretty well. I'm the only one on the ship who can understand him, since he only speaks a few words of English and he comes to me and tells me all his troubles. They call him "third cook," which position covers all the dirty work in the kitchen; and both of the other men jump on him if he peels potatoes when they say to sweep out the pantry and he doesn't understand.

Today was bath day for the gun crew and for some of the rest of us too; the chief petty officer got permission to use the big fire hose, and then he squirted us while we stood stripped, on the iron deck, near the aft hatches.

It was an Adam and Eve affair which I suppose doesn't often happen on the Mauretania or the Espagne. The bath freshened the gunners up so much that they fired four or five practice rounds from the three-inch gun on the stern and a good many more afterwards, from the machine-gun. They aimed at a soap box at several hundred yards, but the ship was rolling so badly they couldn't make a direct hit. They were good shots though, and handled the gun well.

My work after supper this evening might well come under the comic section title, "New Occupations."—This was the pleasant task, when my dishes were done and the pantry floor had been carefully scrubbed and fresh water taken into all the rooms, of teaching the second engineer logarithms. But I shouldn't make a joke out of it. Both of us were in earnest, for he was studying some mathematics relating to his work, and never having had algebra or trigonometry in school, he came to an abrupt stop at logarithms. I wanted to help him; so I got the second mate's book of tables which had all the logs I needed, and we worked two whole hours over it. I had to commence at the very beginning, but he caught on quickly and seemed to have a clear idea of it afterwards.

Smith, the chief wireless operator, gave me two interesting reports to translate today. The first was some French government stuff, from one of the African provinces, I think, and the other was in German and evidently a press report from Berlin. The latter gave a rambling account of the resignation of the Bulgarian consul in Manchester. It commented upon the sinking of a German steamer, and made some absurd statement about a congress being held in Bombay to demand Home Rule for India.

*August 19th.*                        Yea! New York City again.
                                                   But still on the boat.

The watch on the bridge sighted Nantucket light at midnight. At seven this morning we passed Fire Island lightship: then in no time came Sandy Hook, Fort Wadsworth, Quarantine and the battery itself. But the captain got orders, while we were coming up the river, to anchor off the Statue of Liberty instead of going directly to Hoboken as we had intended. It seems we took over about twenty thousand shells by mistake and had to bring them all back again. They must be unloaded on lighters out here in the river, because the law forbids the bringing of such a dangerous cargo into the city docks. I guess all we can do is to sit around here and wait until they finish it. They told me I would be able to get off for good tomorrow.

I was so glad to see the Woolworth building once more that I dumped all the garbage overboard in the North River, when I really shouldn't have; but being actually at New York again, and yet tied up doing dirty mess-boy work on a transport rather irritates me. They wouldn't even let me send a telegram to the family notifying them of my arrival, but I think I can get one through tomorrow morning. The two captains, the chief engineer and the second mate, all went ashore for the evening in the launch. They took several of the crew with them but the mess-boys didn't have a chance. They were very pleasant about it though, and one of them was kind enough to bring back a *Times* and a *Saturday Evening Post*.

*August 21st,* 1917. On Board the Transport *Florence Luckenbach*.
Still opposite the Statue of Liberty.

Things have gone from bad to worse. Even the old Statue of Liberty, which I was so glad to see two days ago, seems to look at me and say, "I'm liberty, all right, but you can't get near me." An immigrant couldn't feel as sore as I do if he were sent back to Europe. For there's nothing wrong with me; they don't need me so much that they couldn't do without me. It's simply that I signed up in St. Nazaire and now they can keep me as long as they want. They have been working two and a half days unloading the shells, and they are not through yet. A gang of longshoremen are doing the work and one of them to whom I gave a sandwich at lunchtime told me they were getting a dollar an hour for this overtime work. He said they made eight or ten dollars a day, on a good job like this.

I don't know when we will get into Hoboken now. Yesterday the captain promised me Wednesday for sure, but now they say we must go into dry-dock in the Erie basin and have a new propeller put on. *Sac à papier*, this is terrible! My family is only sixty miles away, at Bayhead, N. J. I have not received an answer to my telegram yet and don't seem to be able to get in touch with them at all.

# MARCONI WIRELESS TELEGRAPH COMPANY OF AMERICA

Atlantic Ocean _____ Station

45° 21' N - 26° 10' W. _____ Proces-verbal

August 10, 1917

Remarks: German Press Message Probably from Berlin, which was received on the transport. It has been translated as literally as possible by Prof. Priest of Princeton University

8/10/17 -- 11.50 P.M.

☞ Ship Operator

See Chapter 6, Regulation 37 of "General Orders".

Someone is said to have made remarks to the Entente, which are attributed to the former Bulgarian Consul Angelow in Manchester. What worth (there is) in this information proceeds from the fact that after Bulgaria's entrance into the war Angelow ostentatiously gave up his office as Bulgarian Consul, broke off all relations with the Bulgarian Government and with Bulgarian society. If, therefore, Angelow was sent to Stock(holm?) with any commissions, this must have been done only on the part of his friends, but not on the part of the Bulgarian Government, which of course (for the time being) makes no claim to (his) services.

Concerning the fictitious story about the Crown Council which it is said was held at Potsdam on June 5, Count Borchtold (who was), Minister for Foreign Affairs at that time, now declares that according to the assertion of the London "Times," this Crown Council (was held) with the participation of Field-Marshal Archduke Frederick and Chief of the Austro-Hungarian General Staff Baron Conrad and Hungarian Prime Minister Count Tisza.

(In reply to the) utterance of Lloyd George, that the Imperial Chancellor used ambiguous expressions in his explanations of the Reichstag's "Peace Resolution," "Heissmst(?)," points to the explanation of the "North German General News" which cleared up the matter.

The German steamer "Frederick Karo" from Rostock was sunk August 8, going north, off Skelleftea elf in Sweden. According to the report of the pilot the sinking occurred within 800 meters of the Swedish "three mile limit." The foreign vessel which torpedoed the German steamer remained above the surface after accomplishing its act, but bore however no distinguishing features. Newspapers declare this ------ breach of neutrality in regard to food supplies.

A Congress of (East) Indians and committee of Mohammedans held a council together at Bombay, where it was demanded that India (should) at once receive home-rule and have a share in determining her own fate; that, further, India (should) receive a constitution, which is to go into effect immediately after the end of the war, and further, that the English Government's policy of suppression in India must cease at once.

The (well-)known English writer Anna Besant (was) arrested some time ago by English authorities and held captive, as became well known at the Congress of Indians and Mohammedans

*August 23rd.*                      On Board the Crazy *F. L.*
Dry-dock in the Erie Basin.

I enjoy my work more now, with every new day that is added on to our little *repose*. The chamber-maid part is especially delightful. I tuck in the sheets any old way, just so the counterpane covers them, and roll all the pyjamas up in a ball. I guess I won't get the promised tips, but I am so sore at the whole ship I can't sleep. "Bushracks," the ex-steward, has just heard of his brother-in-law's arrest and sentence to two years in jail for bribery in the draft exemption cases. So together we washed away our sorrow with a bowl of grape-juice and pineapple punch which we made secretly in the ice box. (We had borrowed the key unawares some time before.) Ed and I had cleaned it out carefully several days ago and thrown away two hundred pounds of decayed meat. Of course, the place smells queer still: but the punch was excellent.

They say we will be off the boat tomorrow. I don't know what this means. It was to be just one day more when we arrived here last Sunday, and now it's the end of the fifth. Oh Job! Oh Job! I know just how you felt.

The first treat I have had since we arrived came last night when I managed to get off the ship for a couple of hours and, through a telegram sent this morning, met Father at the Waldorf. And I not only did this, but I also called up Bayhead on the phone and talked with my mother and some of the other members of the family for a minute. Father and I and an old friend of the family who happened to be at the hotel took dinner together. It was wonderful to see father again, and I had so much to say about the trip all at once that I could only talk in disconnected sentences. The worst of it all was that I had to go back to the boat again at eleven o'clock. Even then my uniform created quite a lot of excitement in the subway. I hadn't intended wearing it at first, but a quick survey of my wardrobe showed that there was nothing else to do.

This afternoon I managed to get off again for a little while. I saw my brother for a couple of hours before we separated at the Grand Central Station. He was leaving for Fort Niagara to enter the Officers' Training Camp there.

My uniform helps just as much here as it did in London. I have no trouble at all going back and forth through the gates at the Basin. A dignified looking Russian major, thinking that I was a British officer, gave me a fine salute, which of course I returned in front of the hotel.

1. THE EXTERIOR OF A "75" BATTERY. A LARGE SHEET OF CANVAS CONCEALS THE PLACE FROM THE ENEMY WHEN THE GUN IS NOT IN USE.
2. THE INTERIOR OF THE "75" SHELTER. A SHEET OF ARMOUR PLATE PROTECTS THE ARTILLERYMEN FROM ENEMY-FIRE IN FRONT. ON THE LEFT IS A MACHINE FOR SETTING TIME FUSES.
3. A LITTLE FRENCH TOWN IN THE HANDS OF THE ENEMY AND THE TRENCHES LEADING FROM IT. THE DOTS ARE SHELL CRATERS, SOME OF WHICH ARE 30 FEET ACROSS. PHOTOGRAPH TAKEN FROM A FRENCH AEROPLANE AT 10,000 FEET.

1. Bernard Larlenque and the author, at the former's home in Paris. He is just eighteen years old, and a second lieutenant in the French artillery.
2. General G—— of the Alpin Chasseurs with his fourteen different medals.

*August 24th*, 1917.         On a Jersey Central train going home.

My luck changed this morning just as Job's did one day several thousand years ago. We left the dry-dock when I was finishing my rooms and fifteen minutes later were passing the Statue of Liberty. Wasn't I happy when we were actually by her and heading straight for Hoboken! We slid into the pier next to the Vaterland; and all of us waited in tense excitement for news from the captain and his payroll. But none came during the morning, so I got on my uniform, lowered all my luggage over the side by the jib crane, and saw about getting it through the customs before the captain returned. The new crew came on at noon and we didn't have to work at all. The payroll didn't come until four o'clock, but I got thirty-seven dollars and fifty cents out of it, which was worth waiting a few hours for.

Then I said goodbye to all the crew and disappeared down the ladder. Five minutes later I got my last glimpse of the *Luckenbach* from the rear end of an old truck on which my baggage and I were bumping along over the cobble-stones to the Twenty-third Street ferry. After I got over to Manhattan, I checked my luggage from the Jersey Central Station; and now I am on the train home. No more *Luckenbach*, only the family and a quiet time at the seashore for a few weeks. Princeton opens in September and I'll be there with the rest. But next fall it will be France again.

1. The colt machina gun or the stern of the *Luckenbach*.
2. Smith, the wireless operator and "Georgia" Jones, going ashore in the motor boat messboys remain on board. Life-boats are lowered in this manner.
3. Unloading one of our thirty ton guns.
4. Practice with the three inch gun on the *Luckenbach* .

## ALSO FROM LEONAUR
### AVAILABLE IN SOFTCOVER OR HARDCOVER WITH DUST JACKET

**FARAWAY CAMPAIGN** by F. James—Experiences of an Indian Army Cavalry Officer in Persia & Russia During the Great War.

**REVOLT IN THE DESERT** by T. E. Lawrence—An account of the experiences of one remarkable British officer's war from his own perspective.

**MACHINE-GUN SQUADRON** by A. M. G.—The 20th Machine Gunners from British Yeomanry Regiments in the Middle East Campaign of the First World War.

**A GUNNER'S CRUSADE** by Antony Bluett—The Campaign in the Desert, Palestine & Syria as Experienced by the Honourable Artillery Company During the Great War.

**DESPATCH RIDER** by W. H. L. Watson—The Experiences of a British Army Motorcycle Despatch Rider During the Opening Battles of the Great War in Europe.

**TIGERS ALONG THE TIGRIS** by E. J. Thompson—The Leicestershire Regiment in Mesopotamia During the First World War.

**HEARTS & DRAGONS** by Charles R. M. F. Crutwell—The 4th Royal Berkshire Regiment in France and Italy During the Great War, 1914-1918.

**INFANTRY BRIGADE: 1914** by John Ward—The Diary of a Commander of the 15th Infantry Brigade, 5th Division, British Army, During the Retreat from Mons.

**DOING OUR 'BIT'** by Ian Hay—Two Classic Accounts of the Men of Kitchener's 'New Army' During the Great War including *The First 100,000* & *All In It*.

**AN EYE IN THE STORM** by Arthur Ruhl—An American War Correspondent's Experiences of the First World War from the Western Front to Gallipoli-and Beyond.

**STAND & FALL** by Joe Cassells—With the Middlesex Regiment Against the Bolsheviks 1918-19.

**RIFLEMAN MACGILL'S WAR** by Patrick MacGill—A Soldier of the London Irish During the Great War in Europe including *The Amateur Army*, *The Red Horizon* & *The Great Push*.

**WITH THE GUNS** by C. A. Rose & Hugh Dalton—Two First Hand Accounts of British Gunners at War in Europe During World War 1- Three Years in France with the Guns and With the British Guns in Italy.

**THE BUSH WAR DOCTOR** by Robert V. Dolbey—The Experiences of a British Army Doctor During the East African Campaign of the First World War.

AVAILABLE ONLINE AT **www.leonaur.com**
AND FROM ALL GOOD BOOK STORES

# ALSO FROM LEONAUR
### AVAILABLE IN SOFTCOVER OR HARDCOVER WITH DUST JACKET

**THE 9TH—THE KING'S (LIVERPOOL REGIMENT) IN THE GREAT WAR 1914 - 1918** by Enos H. G. Roberts—Mersey to mud—war and Liverpool men.

**THE GAMBARDIER** by Mark Severn—The experiences of a battery of Heavy artillery on the Western Front during the First World War.

**FROM MESSINES TO THIRD YPRES** by Thomas Floyd—A personal account of the First World War on the Western front by a 2/5th Lancashire Fusilier.

**THE IRISH GUARDS IN THE GREAT WAR - VOLUME 1** by Rudyard Kipling—Edited and Compiled from Their Diaries and Papers—The First Battalion.

**THE IRISH GUARDS IN THE GREAT WAR - VOLUME 1** by Rudyard Kipling—Edited and Compiled from Their Diaries and Papers—The Second Battalion.

**ARMOURED CARS IN EDEN** by K. Roosevelt—An American President's son serving in Rolls Royce armoured cars with the British in Mesopotamia & with the American Artillery in France during the First World War.

**CHASSEUR OF 1914** by Marcel Dupont—Experiences of the twilight of the French Light Cavalry by a young officer during the early battles of the great war in Europe.

**TROOP HORSE & TRENCH** by R.A. Lloyd—The experiences of a British Lifeguardsman of the household cavalry fighting on the western front during the First World War 1914-18.

**THE EAST AFRICAN MOUNTED RIFLES** by C.J. Wilson—Experiences of the campaign in the East African bush during the First World War.

**THE LONG PATROL** by George Berrie—A Novel of Light Horsemen from Gallipoli to the Palestine campaign of the First World War.

**THE FIGHTING CAMELIERS** by Frank Reid—The exploits of the Imperial Camel Corps in the desert and Palestine campaigns of the First World War.

**STEEL CHARIOTS IN THE DESERT** by S. C. Rolls—The first world war experiences of a Rolls Royce armoured car driver with the Duke of Westminster in Libya and in Arabia with T.E. Lawrence.

**WITH THE IMPERIAL CAMEL CORPS IN THE GREAT WAR** by Geoffrey Inchbald—The story of a serving officer with the British 2nd battalion against the Senussi and during the Palestine campaign.

AVAILABLE ONLINE AT **www.leonaur.com**
AND FROM ALL GOOD BOOK STORES

www.ingramcontent.com/pod-product-compliance
Lightning Source LLC
Chambersburg PA
CBHW021007090426
42738CB00007B/690